THE MEZCAL EXPERIENCE

A FIELD GUIDE TO THE WORLD'S BEST MEZCALS
AND AGAVE SPIRITS

THE MEZCAL EXPERIENCE

A FIELD GUIDE TO THE WORLD'S BEST MEZCALS AND AGAVE SPIRITS

TOM BULLOCK

jacqui
small

Quarto is the authority on a wide range of topics.

Quarto educates, entertains and enriches the lives of our readers – enthusiasts and lovers of hands-on living.

www.QuartoKnows.com

First published in 2017 by Jacqui Small
An imprint of The Quarto Group
The Old Brewery
6 Blundell St
London N7 9BH, United Kingdom
T (0)20 7700 6700 F (0)20 7700 8066

Publisher: Jacqui Small
Senior Commissioning Editor: Fritha Saunders
Managing Editor: Emma Heyworth-Dunn
Senior Designer: Rachel Cross
Art Director: Penny Stock
Editor: Lucy Bannell
Production: Maeve Healy
Illustrators: Eddie Ruscha Jr; Alberto Cruz Perez
Photography (cocktails): Kim Lightbody
Photography (tasting notes): Simon Murrell
Mixologist: Mark McClintock
Props stylist: Lucy Harvey

ISBN: 978-1-911127-15-4

A catalogue record for this book is available
from the British Library.

2020 2019 2018
10 9 8 7 6 5 4 3 2 1

Printed in China

Please drink responsibly. For the facts, visit drinkaware.co.uk.

CONTENTS

INTRODUCTION
THE JOURNEY

'There is a world beyond ours, a world that is far away, nearby and invisible.'
María Sabina, Mazatec *curandera* and poet

It was 2010 and a newly paved road. Don had been making the same drive for years, slowly navigating boulders and ditches, a drive of six hours, but now we blazed it in three. He pointed out the remains of the old trail, excited when he spotted it from the jeep. He was keen to share and show me what he could. We were on our way to the *palenques* (local distilleries), as they're called in Oaxaca. My first time. The mood of adventure was high.

Our first stop was San Baltazar, Chichicapam, which, as far as I could tell, was a scattering of dwellings studded about a cluster of hills on either side of the road. One of them belonged to Augustin. We pulled in.

It was a compound of sorts. A cement-block house stood at the head of the yard, with a deep, conical stone-lined pit to our left which turned out to be the oven. I was drawn to the oven. It was the central piece and odd. It stood empty, clean – it had just been rebuilt – and its shape, lined with stone, reminded me of skate bowls at skate parks which I've been dropping into all my life.

We stood around the pit and Don explained what we were looking at. Augustin stood close by, quiet but present. Impossibly ancient and striking, Augustin is someone you can't pin an age on. Truly he could be twenty or sixty. This ramped up the sense of timelessness as we stood by his great stone oven, far away in the hills and valleys of the Oaxaqueño highlands.

We were directed around the back of the house into a cool room with bright green walls and a stone floor, where we sat in a circle and – as if bearing witness to a precious sacred rite – silently watched as mezcal was poured for us. There's a picture of me from that morning. I have a small *copita* in one hand, but I don't remember drinking from that. I remember the one

'Welcome to Santa Maria La Pila,
Place of Good Mezcal'

Father and son work together in Miahuatlán, Oaxaca

in my other hand; the huge, wide-rimmed, raw gourd bowl. In the picture I'm drinking from it. It's so large, you can't see my face behind it at all. What a morning.

~

Next stop was San Luis del Rio where a very old fellow named Ignacio makes his mezcal. Made it then, anyway. I hope he still does. We were greeted from the car by his three daughters. Strong, young, pretty, they were in charge. They led us from the road down a trail between fields, straight into the back yard. There was a tin roof, some posts and beams. Beneath them was Ignacio's *palenque*, slightly sunken, dug down into the earth. We climbed in.

Production was on and the stills were kicking. Thick ropes of grey smoke whipped and shrouded the scene. Our eyes stung and poured incessantly. The wood fires flamed beneath the old copper pots; unchanged since eighth-century Persia, they bubbled and clanked, black and green. An enormous man, tall, bald, squarely built, his body thick and seventy years old, limped past me heaving some huge and heavy object, my mind too blown to know what.

Fermentation was deemed complete by the *maestro* and the mash now had to be distilled to avoid altering the flavours from those that he knew he wanted for this batch. Round the clock they would go, seventy-two hours of this. Smoke, fire, sweat, heat. Boggling aromas from the strange brew. Every *palenque* has not only a Virgin de Guadalupe on the wall, but a hammock or an old spring mattress on the floor as well: if the buzz of the mezcal isn't working any more, it's probably best to have a quick lie-down.

We sat down. On a kind of mud couch cut into the side of the *palenque* wall. Someone brought me another gourd bowl, the same size as before — as big as a salad bowl — only this time the mezcal was hot. This was *las primeras quinientas gotas*, or the first five hundred drops. It was so clear, almost like a mirror, perhaps an effect of all the oil. Silver comes to mind.

I was told to sip, but to be careful! This was *puntas*, 'heads', in the high 70 percentages of alcohol by volume; about 150 or 160 proof. I took a sip. Actually a gulp. It started as a sip but it became a gulp. It was delicious. And came with a physical rush that advanced through my body, the physical sensation and the drunk high both, almost exactly at once.

Meanwhile, Ignacio had come in, tiny and bent with an old stick, not, it has to be said, unlike Yoda. Bright-eyed and clearly still strong. He invited us next door into his house. In we went and sat in a sharing silence ramped up by the rocket fuel we'd necked moments before. Ignacio spoke. Don asked if we understood his words. He was talking about the sky, the earth, the rain, *las plantas*. He was really waxing, carried by some animus within. Up he went. I listened intently, not understanding the language but understanding all the same.

Then we were to make our last stop of the day. It was across the river. It hadn't rained for a spell so we could make it — there's no bridge — and Don had some business to do there. It was with Ignacio's two sons.

The view around us was again timeless, serene, still but full of life. We could see far. I'll never forget sitting there at the table. One of the sons – they were in their mid-forties and looked like twins – gave me a bamboo shoot cut at the knuckle and full of mezcal, along with a shot glass to stand the shoot in. I liked that.

Their *palenque* was handsome. Again, sunk into the earth but with much higher ceilings, made of palm leaves. There was more light. Perhaps because they were not in production, it was orderly. Glass flagons stood in rows. Beautiful it looked, really. I have a wonderful picture of one of the sons standing in it. He is very tall. Upright. Everything there had that about it.

~

Eventually it was time to go. You could tell by the light. I felt entirely clear-headed, energized, calmer than I could recall ever feeling before. I didn't want that to stop. Don offered to take us to dinner in Oaxaca City. I cheered. At least silently.

We pulled into the cobbled streets of *centro* and walked in triumph, our return from beyond. We'd seen the other side. We had connected with something so vital and meaningful and brilliant and truly, actually righteous. I could cry recalling how whole it made me feel.

We sat at our table. Don plonked down a five-litre (one-gallon) plastic tub of *puro* right there square in the middle. Job done. Great day. Day one.

~

Whether I found mezcal or it found me, I was especially well prepared to appreciate it when we finally did cross paths. I came to adulthood on a steady diet of, among other things, alcohol and records. And mezcal spoke to all of it.

I started buying records as a kid in the 1970s. I started playing them out in the 1980s and I was producing my own by the time I turned twenty in 1990. My whole life has been submerged in independent record culture and mezcal, for me, pushes all those same buttons.

It speaks to the explorer and the anthropologist digging through the record bins, discovering highly evolved, distinct, regional pockets of creativity. Material made by producers for their communities, proud of their style, decorated with labels that adorn the limited editions with well-considered messages from an ignored and marginalized culture. Objects that are hard to get. And that, when delivered, blow your mind.

~

This is how mezcal had me at first sip. And there has been no turning back. Ten years later, my enthusiasm has led to me being charged with the noble and formidable task of this, trying to document the wide, wide world of mezcal in a book. Whether it is possible is yet to be seen. But I'm certainly not going to turn down the chance to give it a go...

UNKNOWN MEZCAL

'Anyone for a mezcal?'

'A what? You mean the one with the worm?'

The smoke... the worm... the very name. My mum thought I was writing a book about drugs.

~

So, how come all the confusion? Why all the dubious legend and lore? Until very recently, mezcal sat in the public psyche on a par with lost cities, surfacing only in tales of terrifying excess. Footnotes from Hunter S Thompson. A kind of El Dorado of booze.

Few could have imagined that, out there in the lesser-trod pockets of Mexico, one of the world's most distinguished craft delicacies was being unassumingly distilled for the local communities.

So then, what is a mezcal? Well, the answer is not as straightforward as one might hope. In essence, mezcals are Mexican spirits (including tequila) made from agave plants (succulents, not cactae). And that's it.

But, as we look a little closer, we quickly see that it is an unusually elusive subject and difficult to convert to hard fact. The spirit changes its colour from region to region, blending in with the environment. What we're told by one *mezcalero* is often quite different from the words of another. As we move towards it, mezcal seems to retreat. A mirage.

Lumholz, the Danish anthropologist who was, in 1890, the first to document the indigenous peoples of the North-western Sierra Madre (solid mezcal country), titled his book on the subject *Unknown Mexico*. In it, he observed that the shamans of the region, though working with the same spirits, all gave him a different story. The place is mercurial. Unknown Mexico. Unknown mezcal. There's a Mexican expression that is best adopted for the situation. *Lo unico que sé, es que no se nada.* 'The only thing I know, is that I know nothing.' A good place to start.

This book is a guide; nothing can teach us better than the mezcal itself. But I hope it will give you what you need to best receive those teachings. It is a guide to assist you in the field of your own discoveries. Take it with you, to the *mezcalerias*, to the *palenques*, and may it serve you well.

Tom Bullock, Mexico City, January 2017

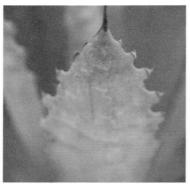

WORK
CREATE
TEACH
RESPECT
ENJOY
SUSTAIN

THE MEZCAL PARADOX

Like all the best things in life, mezcal, at its heart, is full of paradox.

It is, at once, both ceremonial and fun. It's used as a medicine but, if you're not careful, gets you royally wasted. It's for the everyday, while being rather special.

It comes from an indomitable culture, thousands of years old, that has permeated most corners of the planet, yet no one seems to have heard of it.

Currently, it is baffling sommeliers and celebrity chefs everywhere with the possibilities offered by its sophistication. While back home in Mexico, it's being made with the most rustic and rudimentary set-ups possible.

In the flavours themselves, we find ourselves oscillating between poles, lost in some yin and yang of taste. Subtle shades of sweetness… or are those bitter sours? Flowers meet plimsolls in a new logic that – somehow – all makes perfect sense.

How is this possible? Even the effects seem to work all ways at once. Calming while stimulating. We're composed and wonderfully loose all at the same time.

¡REVOLUTION!

For much of its life, mezcal has been misunderstood. It's been the underdog, the outsider. For many Mexicans it has come to be associated only with the rural South and peasant culture; while choosing the tequilas and industrial spirits of the North was to affiliate with romantic and aspirational ideas of Old Spain and 'the West'. Mezcal found itself marginalized and derided.

Though a surprising number of Mexicans still think of mezcal as 'the one with the worm that'll make you go blind', the tables are slowly beginning to turn. A change of perception is starting to sweep the nation and with it comes a great deal of pride.

It began with the upper-middle classes who, as part of the global trend towards returning to craft culture, became aware of the value and abundance of their own heritage. Mezcal specifically, through its very nature, seemed to create a bridge between the classes where before the gap had seemed impossible to span.

'Mezcal is the only real revolution,' says Ulises Torrentera of In Sítu, a *mezcaleria* in Oaxaca that serves some of the finest mezcals in Mexico. And he's right. After centuries of conflict, mezcal is bringing Mexican people together in a way the country's other revolutions had failed to do.

But while the nation is celebrating its quintessentially Mexican global treasure, familiar forces of corruption and industry are starting to creep in. Mezcal's long story has just reached the world stage. It is a brand-new beginning. How will it play out?

CULTURE AND HISTORY

MYTH BUSTING

Mezcal is a community-based, highly regional craft culture. The communities that make it, that have managed to continue making it, in the traditions they developed over time, are rural and – at their heart – indigenous. Let's zoom out...

Mexico, when the Spanish conquistadors arrived, was made up of many different people, some twenty-four million of them, speaking one hundred and eighty languages. That was only five hundred years ago. And a great many of those cultures have survived the pressures (to put it mildly) of colonialization and are very much alive today. There are, for example, sixteen languages spoken in Oaxaca alone. Like a language, mezcal – along with textiles, food, pottery and music – forms a cultural identity for the people. It is theirs, it is them, they are proud of it.

I have met many *mezcaleros* who haven't visited other mezcal-producing communities for decades. Why would they? They have what they need, their traditions work and – as they have fought so hard to preserve them – they are resistant to change. This has meant little sharing of practices from one village to the next. This strength of identity is why one mezcal is very different from another. And why an outsider was, until now, rarely going to get a taste of any of them. Which, in an ethnically divided Mexico, led to rumour and superstition. And from that came lore.

THE WORM

The mezcal worm, or *gusano*, also has plenty of paradox. It's faintly comical, but a serious problem. It's gross to look at, but tastes quite good. And it's a love-hate relationship for the hard-working *agaveros*. They are part of a bizarre food chain. The worm – in fact a larva that will turn into a moth called *Hypopta agavis* – feeds on the agave. Which is bad news for the farmer, but he in turn eats the worm as it's highly nutritious. It can be gobbled whole or served in tacos, or dried, ground up, mixed with chilli (chile) and salt, sprinkled on top of a slice of orange as *sal de gusano* and served with mezcal.

The worm can also be dropped whole into a bottle, either to mask lousy flavours or to enhance a fine mezcal with a delicate fungal vibe. The practice appears to have got a little out of control, however, during the mid-twentieth-century, when a brand called Gusano Rojo tried to make a name for itself by popping one in every single bottle, prompting Monte Alban to follow suit. Which led to a prolonged and groovy advertising campaign printed in innumerable issues of 1970s *Playboy* that cemented the idea in the male Western mind that this was in fact the real mezcal. Amazing how tenacious a bad idea can be.

Building the tapada *while the oven is lit*

THE SMOKE

Mezcal is known to many people as 'the smoky one'. And for those people the smoke is thought to be a bit much. But there are many craft mezcals with no smoke at all (see Viejo Indecente, page 182) and a lot of my favourites are balanced in such a way that the smoke flavour is subtle and complementary.

Perhaps the confusion lies with the majority of exported mezcals, until recently, being massive on smoke and big on peats, to cater to the assumed flavour preferences of the American market. A situation reminiscent of the California wine craze of the 1990s when it was all chardonnays with 'big oak'; again, a style that proved controversial and far from universally popular. We can call this, mezcal's version, 'big smoke', a myth that will hopefully dissipate rather than be played up for promotion like the *gusano*. In reality, the smoke flavour is a precisely controlled part of production and should arrive to the drinker in pleasant harmony with all the mezcals' other flavours.

IT'LL MAKE YOU HALLUCINATE

The first mention of mezcal I ever caught was in reference to its purported power to make you trip. Or, more specifically, that eating the worm after finishing the bottle would bring on this effect. Which, even as a gormless teen, I knew must be rubbish, because anyone drinking that much alcohol was bound to see colours, or to be so drunk as to think they did, a fact that would also be evident in their willingness to eat worms.

Perhaps the confusion here lies in etymology. 'Father Peyote' is a Mexican psychotropic cactus. A person under its influence appears drunk. In the eighteenth century, Spanish colonists chose to call that cactus the 'mezcal bean'. So when, years later, during scientific analysis of the cactus, the psychotropic ingredient was found, it was called 'mescaline'. But it's nothing to do with mezcal.

~

However, I feel there is a kernel of truth that seeded this legend. Drinking mezcal gives one an undeniably lucid feeling that is unique to the spirit. We don't feel the flushed grogginess of wines, or the glare and dip of whisky and gin. We get 'high', so to speak. With mezcal, the elevator is going straight up. It is stimulating, energizing (some suggest this is due to the sugars being structurally distinct agave sugars) and, in moments I have personally experienced, subtly hallucinogenic. (See Pare de Sufrir, page 128.)

For me, these moments have been at first sip, which negates the idea of it being some kind of brain collapse due to excess alcohol. I immediately experienced a very mild, benign — but definitely heightened — awareness outside of what would be described as our usual, daily functioning levels of consciousness.

TEQUILA

I'm often asked, 'What's the difference between tequila and mezcal?' And I often watch the questioner's eyes slowly glaze over as I waffle into detail about the – to me – fascinating social, economic and technical factors that have made the two drinks unique in their own right.

When perhaps what I could simply say is that tequila is a kind of mezcal in the way that Bordeaux is a type of wine. And that they are not different but the same. Mezcal is the name for all agave spirits and tequila is just one sort. And this, in essence, *is* the answer. But, as we shall see, on the ground, it's far more complicated than that.

In a nutshell then, tequilas, only a hundred or so years ago, tasted much like great mezcals do today. They were produced more or less the same way and were made with many different types of agave, as mezcals still are. Today, however, only one type of agave is used, the *Agave azul*. And through technological 'advances' that increase production, tequilas have become more exacting and predictable in their flavours and expression.

A laboratory in Tequila looks on to a row of 80,000-litre (18-gallon) fermentation tanks. Technical 'advances' in production increase volume and revenue but at a cost to the expression of the spirit

ROOTS AND LEGENDS

THE PULQUE CULT

From Jalisco to Oaxaca, Tamaulipas to Guerrero, all regions of mezcal culture share a common root in the distant past: an understanding of agave as deity. We're all the children of Mayahuel.

Last year, my daughter persuaded me to take us to Teotihuacán. I'll forever be indebted. As we trekked along the Avenue of the Dead, from the Pyramid of the Sun to the Pyramid of the Moon, much of what I had been absorbing for ten years on the subject of mezcal, sip by sip and word for word, seemed to fall into place. It all lined up like the ancient city itself.

Teotihuacán, known as the Birthplace of the Gods and, not quite so epically, as The Belly Button of the World, was built two thousand years ago, in the midriff of Mexico, the very centre of the Americas: North, Central and South. (How did they know?) At that time, most of us in Britain were living in humble homes of wood and mud. Teotihuacán, on the other hand, had multi-storied, intricately decorated luxury apartments. Even today, it still feels metropolitan. The central road, three miles long, stretches out like some Fifth Avenue, offering temples instead of department stores.

Mapped with great technical skill to the movements of the planets, Teotihuacán was fuelled by *pulque*, fermented agave nectar. *Pulque* was the electricity that powered the city.

Pulque is still enjoyed today, in bars in Mexico City and across the country. By carving a bowl into the crown of certain agaves, sap is caused to secrete into the carving, and is collected. This nectar is called *aqua miel* and is delicious. When fermented, it becomes milky, slightly fizzy and mildly alcoholic and a cup gives you a zingy buzz. If you drink a lot of it, which in Teotihuacáno ritual was the order, things get all kinds of jazzy. To Mesoamerican people, it was direct communication with the agave deity, Mayahuel, the holiest of sacraments. Agaves were yet to be used to make spirits, but the journey to mezcal had begun.

RABBIT'S MOON

Ten thousand years prior to Teotihuacán's construction, migration across the Bering Straits had brought the first inhabitants to Mexico. There they inherited the agave. They had lucked out, and they knew it. They ascribed a deity to the plant: Mayahuel. She was fertility. She gave life.

From her came mother's milk, the white nourishing *pulque* that fed the 400 animal gods that were her offspring. Each had a name and a myth. These were white rabbit creatures, mischievous and humorous, Puckish and magnetic. Quite remarkable is how strongly their stories echo myths and legends from elsewhere around the world.

The Sun Temple at Teotihuacán

Seeing white rabbits, and relating them to phenomena that occur beyond the perimeter of our everyday lives, appears to be a universal vision. In the West we have the rabbit that Alice follows down the rabbit hole to a place where reality is turned on its head. Japanese, Chinese, Buddhist and Native American cultures all have much-loved myths of the rabbit in the moon. Stories not of daylight – in which we know where we stand – but visions in moonlight… where anything goes.

These ideas lend weight to a theory from the bottler of Mi Chingón (see page 164). Karl Lenin suggests that the root of the word 'mezcal' is more profound than the translation we are familiar with now. Mezcal is a Nahuatl word, made up of three pictographic symbols:

Metl – 'agave'   **Ixca** – 'cooked'   **Calli** – 'house'

Combined, this is thought to mean 'agave cooked in an earth oven'. It seems a little too literal, appealing to modern thinking. It's also misspelt. Mezcal, in its oldest form, is spelt with a 'z'.

If we take the *spelling* literally, which seems wise, we get something quite different.

Metl – 'agave'   **Zee** – 'white' and/or 'moon'   **Calli** – 'house'

Mezcal becomes 'agave in the house of the moon', much more in tune with the poetic language and the mythology of the people who first made mezcal and the aura that surrounds the drink.

THE FIRST
DISTILLERS

WHO STARTED IT?

It's into the mad unknown of a new world and the chaos of a fallen kingdom that mezcal first emerges. Hardly any wonder as it's safe to say that everyone needed a drink. Cortés had arrived from Spain and defeated the Aztec empire. Both sides were scrambling for certainties. For the Aztecs, their deities had been dashed, their pantheon of gods and goddesses rendered seemingly useless. While for Cortés and his men, it's hard to imagine what depths of faith they would have had to call on to face such unlikely odds and shocking otherness.

But was it, as is so commonly assumed, the conquistadors who distilled *las primeras quinientas gotas*, seizing upon local fermentations, brandishing a copper alembic and applying what some popular fellow in the band knew of brandy distillation?

Many argue that the indigenous people had already worked it out. After all, they'd mastered enough to make contemporary Spain look, well, medieval. But there is also strong and somewhat surprising evidence that it may have been Filipino sailors who, having brought their stills and skills to Mexico aboard the Manila galleon in the 1570s, may have distilled the first mezcal.

Upon arrival in Mexico, Filipinos established coconut plantations along the West coast. Here, using techniques mastered back home, they made a spirit called *lambanog* by distilling fermented coconut mash. Studies point to the origins of mezcal production taking firm hold along the coast beneath the Colima volcanos, right where the coconut palms grew.

Maybe it was all of the above. Each camp remote and quite unaware of the other working it out, little by little. It seems likely. There is, after all, evidence of native distillation prior to the conquest, only not using agaves. But for me, that is enough; the chances are high that some wise old wonder gave distilling his *tepache* (fermented cooked agave) a try using techniques that are still in use today.

Those who oppose this idea cite the lack of contemporary documentation on the subject, and in a land where writing was popular and evolved, that does seem surprising. Only the conquistadors systematically destroyed much of that. Or perhaps, through fear of persecution, any records were hidden by the *mezcaleros* themselves.

The very first record of a mezcal is from 1619 and it is a prohibition levied against production by the Castilian crown. Mezcal, still wet behind the ears, was already outlawed.

Agave azul 'Weber' *in the fields of La Alteña, Arandas, Jalisco. Notice the iron-rich red soil of the region*

RUN TO THE HILLS

UNDER THE VOLCANO – CLANDESTINE CULTURE

Mezcal, though often finding itself on the wrong side of the law, has always been popular. And this was a frustration for the government of New Spain, which expected its colony to provide financial returns, not only from its natural resources, but from what could be sold back to its subjects. Not least in the way of booze. Spain was importing wine and brandy and, if these agave spirits could not be stamped out, they would at least be controlled.

~

In the North, mezcal producers were given sanction under the watchful eye of the landlords of the haciendas, all the better for drawing maximum financial return. (It is said that the nave of the cathedral of Guadalajara was paid for in mezcal!) But in the South, where resistance to colonial incursion remained intense, mezcal distillation remained independent.

It did this on the down-low. And in the cat-and-mouse games that were to follow for centuries to come, there were a number of factors to mezcal's advantage. Mezcal, for one, was mobile. The only kit that need be transported was copper pans. The rest – a trunk for the still; water to cool the evaporated alcohol; wood for the fire; pits that could be covered and hidden during fermentation; and the agave – was all in abundance in the wild. When tipped off to a constable (police officer) on horseback, scanning the landscape for give-away smoke, the *mezcalero* could pack up and swiftly dip into the next valley, or hide in the hills and wait it out. This is what gave the distilleries their name *palenque*, meaning 'clearing': clearings in the wild.

~

There were other things going for the early bootlegger. The closed communities of the South were quite able, through organized communication, to keep what they wished under wraps. There are thrilling accounts of mezcal smugglers, many of them women, who, under less suspicion than men, braved random checks to get the mezcals door-to-door or surreptitiously out to market where they were sold under the table.

But, ultimately, the greatest power rural mezcal-making communities had was one that could never be stamped out: the belief that mezcal was a sacred expression of the old gods; a medicine they had divinely inherited. This belief kept the culture we experience today wholly intact. While the properties of the mezcal, in turn, gave them the strength to believe.

Though they persisted – it was still illegal to make mezcal in Sonora, Guerrero and Michoacán right into the mid-1990s – the authorities were never going to win.

Simple tools for preparing good mash

THE GREAT DIVIDE

MEZCAL AND TEQUILA PART WAYS

During the century leading up to the revolutionary war, Tequila became the most highly developed region of mezcal production. A number of enterprising *tequileros* wrested free of the old-school landlord hacienda systems that had given sanction to mezcal production, slipped from the hills and went private back in town, namely Tequila town and Arandas. They had a tad more loot, which enabled them to invest in new tech ideas to increase their output.

Meanwhile, the new nation of Mexico, free (falling) from its bonds with Old Spain was, itself, keen to invest in new ideas. Victory in the War of Independence of 1810 had been a bit of a shock. What now?! Very few had expected to win. The stuffy generals and ageing priests who took the reins of the nascent Federal Republic, looking for inspiration, were quickly charmed by the burgeoning new industry in Europe, particularly Britain. Blinded by a shiny vision of a bright industrial future, government, in league with business, copied European templates, costing the field labourer his common rights and the artisan his craftsman's status.

Revolutionary forces at the start of the Mexican Revolution, 1910

Copper column stills in use today in Arandas, Jalisco

Before long, through the ingenuity of a certain Martin Martinez de Castro, the town of Tequila was looking at the dials, pipes, levers and hatches of a fantastic, Jules Verne-esque, towering copper column still. In 1890, stone masonry ovens (*mamposteria*) were built to replace the ancient earth pit *hornos*. These enabled more agave to be cooked in less time. The industry was ready to make some serious volume. Tequila was becoming tequila with a small 't'.

Which, 20 years later, was good news for the armed forces of the Mexican Revolution. To win a war, you need courage. And there's not much that delivers that more than a shot of mezcal. After 1910, there wasn't a soldier who went into the darker stages of the Revolution without a *canuté*, a bamboo shoot, swinging from a cord about his neck, holding a dose of what we now, in most cities around the world, sip, covet and intellectualize at our local *mezcaleria*.

'*¡Para todo mal, mezcal, y para todo bien, también!*' Indeed. For consolation, for celebration, or simply as an early equivalent of a military morphine shot, mezcal was crucial. It was clear that more would be needed to stay the course. So much so that the lines of tequila production needed to be increased, essentially industrialized. Tequila took to the task, set their new innovations to maximum and jumped production to unprecedented levels.

This is the fork in the road. Or the fork that drives the road apart. Mezcal, as we still know it, and tequila, as it was fast becoming, in the midst of the chaos and confusion of war, part ways. It would be another hundred years until they'd begin to see eye-to-eye again.

THE BUSINESS OF MODERN TEQUILA

DENOMINATION OF ORIGIN: MOVING THE GOAL POSTS

In 2012, just before she died, the legendary *ranchera* singer most intimately associated with tequila country, Chavela Vargas, was given a bottle of mezcal by *mezcalera* Karla Moles. Upon presenting the bottle, Karla apologized, pointing out that it was mezcal and not tequila. 'No my dear, that's quite all right,' the singer said, 'There's no more tequila left. We drank it all!'

The takeaway from this anecdote is, for me, the diva's recognition that much of the tequila available now is not what it used to be. It's been drained of its character and, as one artisanal tequila producer puts it, of 'its agave soul'.

~

Tequila's road from prized local mezcal to giant international industrial spirit has been long and problematic. And those problems – for producers, for farmers and for the flavours themselves – seem to lie in the Denomination of Origin and the very agreements and institutions that were put in place to protect the drink and its culture in the first place.

Denominations of Origin stem from a system of *appellations* introduced in France during the nineteenth century to regulate and protect the wine industry. The objective of a DO is to protect a product's quality, but also the culture surrounding it: its people.

~

After a series of standards that helped to define the individuality of the spirit in 1974, tequila won its own DO. But immediately, there was controversy. For example, the borders of what was considered the region of tequila were absurdly extended to accommodate political ambitions hundreds of miles away. Even to places that had never had anything to do with it, as far away as Tamaulipas, a desert state on the other side of the country. Not an auspicious start, by anyone's reckoning.

In the decades to come, blights from over-farming and further industrial/political manoeuvring – coupled with the introduction of mechanical equipment that could dramatically further the kind of productivity needed to meet market demand – powerfully drained tequila of its original character. Distressingly, these are now the kinds of dangers that the other regions of mezcal culture face as they emerge on to the world's stage. The question is: can we do better this time around?

Mezcal is based in spiritual life. The two are inseparable for mezcal-making communities

MEZCAL'S CHALLENGE

THE MEZCAL NOM AND COMERCAM

In 1994, mezcal received its own Denomination of Origin, NOM-070-SCFI-1994. In 1997, a governing body was set up to oversee its application: the COMERCAM or, if you like, Consejo Mexicano Regulador de la Calidad del Mezcal. Today, COMERCAM is simply called the CRM, or el Consejo Regulador de Mezcal. Its headquarters are in Oaxaca and it has its work cut out for it.

Typically, a DO is ascribed to the way a region makes a specific item: the way the French make cheese in Roquefort, say, or a wine in Bordeaux. But mezcal (unlike Tequila) is not a place. It is mezcal – the entire category and every region of the enormous country in which it is made – that the CRM is trying to accommodate in its rule book of protection. Which is, frankly, not something likely to work well.

But the CRM does offer a way to join a growing market. Producers who are registered and find a brand to work with report that, though the paperwork makes life complicated, they feel positive about the changes it enforces. They are excited to display their talents on the world stage where their craft, the real agave spirits, can at last be appreciated alongside the other great spirit traditions of the world. At the same time, the CRM suggests that it is safeguarding the industry from low-quality spirits, thus protecting its international reputation and also protecting the traditions used to make it.

Honourable intentions… that some consider misguided at best. Hugo D'Acosta, who has been involved with craft mezcal since the 1990s, suggests that the CRM is going the wrong way about carrying out its mission. He argues that, to protect the culture, we should be concentrating on logging 'practices handed down from generation to generation, now, before they disappear'. He also feels that the CRM should concentrate on protecting both plants and farming techniques.

Meanwhile, the complexities of registering are found to be prohibitive to most. Furthermore, there are some producers who would simply rather not, thanks very much. They know that their inherited recipes won't make the overly stringent measures required to comply with CRM standards, and are content to keep producing, as they always have, for their community.

Then there are other producers who cannot register even if they wanted to. Producers who woke up one day to find that, for arbitrary reasons, their *palenque* was in the wrong municipality to even be included in the NOM. Twenty-four of the thirty-one states of Mexico can prove a history of mezcal production – the principal qualification for inclusion – but only nine states are in the DO. These are the sort of problems the CRM and the producers are coming up against as they attempt to shoehorn 'mezcal' into a box that can be shipped abroad. Meanwhile, the commercialization of mezcal is doing fine with the new parameters and blazing ahead whether anyone likes it or not.

WHAT'S ON THE LABEL?

NOM 70: BLENDED SPIRITS AND 'ARTISANAL' MEZCALS

There's something particularly satisfying about pouring a mezcal from an unbranded clear bottle. The sense that we're really in the thick of it; under the radar and closer to the source. Probably because we are.

Few of the branded mezcals are exactly how we'd find them in a mezcal-making community. Unfettered, a producer brings a mezcal to measure in response to whatever the circumstances happen to be during production: the weather; the qualities of the plants and how they responded in fermentation and the still; even his mood (see page 70 for more about this process). The result will be different each time, whereas most brands have a set recipe and they and the *mezcalero* have an agreement to bring it to the same exact ABV and flavour profile each time.

Fortunately, there are some brands where the whole reason they exist is to bring you just what is happening at the source. Brands like Real Minero, for example. And thrillingly, the market for these mezcals is increasing with the number of brands wishing to do the same thing.

~

But, just as we draw closer to this goal, the goal posts are being whisked away. Yesterday, on 23 February 2017, the Norma Oficial Mexicano – or NOM 70 – was, with little fanfare, finally pushed through by the CRM. It had been an awfully long time coming and many of the measures that brands had been pushing for were addressed; most significantly, the creation of classifications that distinguish one mezcal from another.

The NOM details what can be classified as 'mezcal', 'artisanal mezcal', or 'ancestral mezcal'. But the classifications leave out as much as they put in and the idea that they will be able to establish quality, rather than just qualities, is incorrect. Yes, going forward, an industrial plant – pumping out thousands of litres (gallons) of spirits a week, made of 49% sugar cane – is no longer able to sell their spirit under the same name as a small batch, hand-crafted clay-pot spirit made from wild-grown agaves. But that is enough to assure the hope for protection to the traditional practices.

~

What is not mentioned, however – along with whether ambient yeasts or processed yeasts need to be used, a glaring omission, and how many *grados* constitute an authentic mezcal – is 'blends'. A brand can collect batches from sources hard to monitor, lump them together and call them 'artisanal'.

Can this be an oversight? This not only leaves room, but gives sanction, to individuals with big business models to take advantage. Those brands struggling to bring genuine mezcal to the public at an accessible price face being undermined and unable to compete with those making blends and, well, why on Earth should they?

We find ourselves at a point where we all – brand owners, producers and consumers alike – have to ask whether we'd all be better off leaving the so-called mezcals to the mainstream and instead embracing the new name given to mezcals *outside* the NOM: Aguardiente de Agave.

AGUARDIENTE DE AGAVE

The classifications of NOM 70 are – to thousands of Mexican mezcal producers – never to be applicable. They are, after all, only for those who are, or can be, registered in the first place, which is a fraction of those who traditionally make it. Furthermore, it is prohibitive in a new kind of way for many who could actually register. Why go through all the bother only to be lumped in with the other, much cheaper, mass-produced industrial spirits being called 'mezcal'? It makes it hard to compete even if you felt you wanted to.

~

A little madly, the Mexican government has claimed the word 'mezcal' as its intellectual property. From now on, any unregistered mezcal must be called *Aguardiente de Agave*, essentially meaning 'agave hooch'. Not great, but what has not been accounted for is how this pointed thrust in one direction leaves a gaping opportunity in the other. Why even play ball? There are, at this time, many more *mezcaleros* and *mezcaleras* unregistered than there are registered. Their Aguardiente de Agave, it can be argued, is a more honest representation of actual mezcal culture, and much better booze to boot. Either way, all this doesn't make it a lot easier to know which to choose. It helps to know what to look for on those labels.

~

A 40% ABV mezcal is made for the foreign market. Some are 'single village', however, and carry more character, weight and girth than others. While finding a bottle at 45% and up, you're starting to play ball. Truly traditional mezcals rarely come in below 46% and, more often than not, hover about 50% and higher. This is because they're not watered down and the adjustments needed to find the sweet-spot for well-balanced flavours are easier to make without the stringent – and largely unnecessary – rules for acidity, for example. (The exception might be a 'single' distillation made during the cold season, when fermentation has not produced a great deal of alcohol, bringing the spirit in around the low 40s.) The higher the ABV, the more oils there are in the distillate. These oils carry an abundance of rich flavours and create deep complexity. They're precious. You don't water them down unless you have to.

How much was produced of a particular mezcal is another way to read authenticity. Fifty litres (eleven gallons) indicates a rarer plant or process and, before mezcal became noticed overseas, there was rarely any need for higher volume from a batch or a *palenque*.

A label that carries the production information says good things. The producer, the region, the plant, the process. If a label shows this, it's because it matters. It's not a blend.

Beyond that, it's just like it was back in the day, digging for records before the .com. You have to know your stuff and you learn what to look for. Certain labels (brands) and producers (*maestros*). From certain places (regions), featuring certain musicians (plants). It's a big part of the fun. Especially when you get it home, put it on and it's a banger.

'We will not adapt to this system'

PLANTS

THE PRECIOUS
AGAVE

'O f no other plant is there such abundance in New Spain. If people would learn to live in moderation and balance, as is reasonable, this plant would be sufficient to supply all human needs, for the benefits and uses that come from it are almost innumerable.' The words of Francisco Hernández in the 1570s, describing what he called *el árbol de las maravillas*. Though we now know that agaves are succulents of the same family as asparagus (of all things), his enthusiastic description of them as 'the tree of marvels' rings true. Their ability to provide for the animal kingdom, mankind and themselves is to be marvelled at.

Its talents were not lost on Carl Linnae, the Dane known as the father of modern botany. In 1753, he named the plant the 'agave', after the Greek deity of nobility. Notably, she was also mother to Dionysus – god of ritual madness – and the specific species he christened was *Agave americana*, already, at that time, producing great mezcals. Prior to Linnae, the agave was known by its Antillean name, the *maguey*. In Mexico, where it is native and more than half the total recorded number of species grow exclusively, it was known by many names, and identified as comprising many species. It was – and still is to some – a sacred plant.

~

If you walk in the wilds of Mexico, shoulder to shoulder among agave, growing where they will, you realize that they are special. Their singular blue-green iridescence marks them out as something unique in the landscape, somehow more alive than the scrub that grows about them.

They are individuals, characters, independent (literally, as some reproduce non-sexually), but also part of our community; is there another plant, anywhere, that provides so much?

The gear list is long. The *cuioté*, for one, makes a solid but light trunk that's good for beams in construction and furniture. The leaves, hardened, make tiles for roofing, while their fibres make durable rugs, baskets, shoes, or are woven to make fabrics; the thorns providing needles, already attached to the thread. Those seriously strong thorns also work as nails and formidable arrowheads. Agave gives us soaps and shampoos, jewellery, balms and medicines. On it goes like some mad wonder. As the great ethnobotanist, Howard Scott Gentry, whose life's work was dedicated to the agave, said, 'The uses for agaves are as many as the arts of man have found it convenient to devise.' And after housing us and clothing us and arming us and cleaning us, they feed us as well. Then, of course, there are the drinks.

A vast Arroqueño *yet to reach maturity*

Sin maguey no hay mezcal. ¡Si, claro! It is the agaves, after all, that make it mezcal and what makes it so Mexican. The genus began life in Mexico ten million years ago. Now, there are two hundred and eight known species of agave. Though there are certainly many more out there. Mezcaleros discover them all the time.

But how many are being used to make mezcal is not clear. Perhaps around fifty, but from the most zealous bar-nerd to the head of COMERCAM, everyone admits it's an unknown.

As with much of mezcal's story, the mystery is brought on by Mexico's intense regionality. Not only is there little interaction between mezcal-making communities, but the languages they confer in are typically super-regional dialects. So, what is a madrecuishe in Miahuatlán is called a cirial some thirty miles away in Matatlán. Or a tripon only twenty miles from there in Santa Catarinas. These are all variants of one species known scientifically as Agave karwinskii. Sometimes, however, two agaves of a completely different species share the same name. A verde in Oaxaca is a type of karwinskii; while a verde in Durango is a form of Agave durangensis. It's mercurial stuff, but it's half the fun of being a mezcal explorer.

Another reason why it's so tricky to pin down what's what is that the agave is botanically 'promiscuous'. It will easily cross-pollinate and form new varieties. When Mexico's nomadic early inhabitants found properties to one agave that were of use, they would uproot that plant and carry it along with them (there is a technique of cutting the central leaf to make a shoulder strap). At the next camp they replanted it, where it would promptly cross-pollinate with local species, creating new forms of plants and marrying their characteristics and human uses.

~

On the subject of uses, mezcal has, since its inception, been seen and used as a medicine. Externally, for a cold or a fever, mezcal is rubbed into the temples and applied to the feet. The cooling effect is soothing while the mezcal also enters the blood stream and is thought to help recovery. A more exaggerated version, I was told, involves holding a child with a cold, covering their eyes, then spraying a mouthful of mezcal over them for the same effect. I don't doubt it, though I don't think I'll try it.

Mezcal taken internally is always more fun and plants thought to hold healing properties, of which Mexico has a wide range, were and still are kept in mezcal to make an infusion for drinking known as a curado. Garlic for colds, for example, or lemon verbena for menstrual cramps, or marijuana for overall wellbeing.

Mural in the school playground, Mitla, Oaxaca

THE SEX LIFE OF AN AGAVE

Agave plants are, by anyone's standards, masters of design. Not only do they provide for us, they look after themselves very well, too. Formidably armed with spikes and toxicity to drive off the most determined animal foragers, they also continue their sapline in a surprising number of ways. These are exploited by the *agavero* to create a healthy supply for mezcal production.

One way is, of course, through seeds. When an agave has reached full maturity, it concentrates all the energy in its body and slowly starts to push, up through the central rosette of its body, a thick, rather phallic trunk called the *cuioté*. The *cuioté* grows swiftly at around one foot every month and to an admirable height of some twenty or thirty feet. At the tip of the trunk sprouts the candelabra, a chandelier-like collection of flowers and seed pods. From that height the seeds can scatter far and wide. It also keeps them safely out of the way of predators while, at the same time, in the path of pollinators: birds and insects in the day; nocturnal, nectarivorous and blood-sucking vampire bats at night.

~

An agave plant, as well as creating seeds and pollen, also generates basal shoots, though *mezcaleros* call them – more charmingly – *hijuelos* or *hijos*: children. Stand next to an agave in the wild and you will see a dozen or so baby clones mushrooming up around their mother's feet.

Another method is to generate aerial rosettes. The *mezcaleros* call them *magueyitos* – 'baby maguey' – and they are produced in the flowering stalks at the crown of the *cuioté*. When finally released from the stem pods, they fall, ready-formed, to the earth: tiny agaves, looking to root. These can be collected and planted wherever the *agavero* chooses.

And, if this was not enough, there's even an axillary shoot that sprouts a whole new plant right out of the agave's midriff! Left to their own devices, they are simply unstoppable.

SILVESTRES

Silvestres are agaves that grow and are harvested in the wild. The word has origins in the name of the Roman deity, Silvanus, meaning 'of the woods', who presided over the plants and trees, held them precious and worked to preserve and protect their wild nature.

~

Until the last hundred years or so, all agaves used for making mezcal grew where they naturally took to the conditions in the wild. The *magueyero* would gather all maguey suitable for production, indiscriminate of species, for sale to the *mezcaleros*. Or, particularly in the South, where producers remained mobile to avoid taxes or prohibitions, *mezcaleros* themselves would move to an area of open land, set up their still and harvest all the *silvestres* in reach.

Seeds

Bulbos

A nursery of tepaztate, *Oaxaca*

Once they'd cleared the area of usable plants, they'd move on to the next spot, slowly rotating through the region to return years later, by which time other agaves had reached maturity.

With industrialization in Jalisco in the nineteenth century, followed by an increased demand for mezcal in the 1930s, the practice of farming agaves began to intensify. *Agave tequilano*, aka *Agave azul*, and the *Agave angustafolia*, or *espadin*, were the obvious choices. Not only do both grow faster than other species (the *Agave tequilano* being, in fact, a variant of *espadin*), and yield more sugars and hence more mezcal, but they also respond more easily to cultivation. All other species, which were soon to become known as *silvestres*, were left to grow as they were, as it wasn't economical to farm them.

All the same, in Oaxaca, where there was less industry, a single batch of mezcal might be made from as many as ten or twenty different species, while a mezcal of a single variety as we are used to today would have been very unusual.

~

In 1996, Ron Cooper, mezcal pioneer and owner of Del Maguey (see page 142), came across a producer making this kind of mezcal in Oaxaca. The producer, for personal reasons, had chosen to make a mezcal solely of the small and highly prized *tobalá* agave. Cooper was struck not only by the exquisite taste, but from seeing the way that – produced this way – mezcal could demonstrably mirror a wine: with varietals.

It was a breakthrough. And, in the international market, it proved an effective way of suggesting mezcal's unique qualities. It was also a step towards sharpening our understanding of how terroir was playing a role in production. In many ways, a win-win. Though, in time, this would create unprecedented pressure on the maguey. Species millions of years old were being asked to change the way they live, grow and reproduce.

~

At this moment, hundreds of thousands of young *silvestres* sit in greenhouses, awaiting transplantation. As the plants take so long to mature, there are very few examples of how these once wild, farmed *silvestres* are going to respond to their new life. Tequila's *Agave azul*, for example, has had a very hard time of it.

I was told by tequila historian Juan Bernardo Torres that there were once thirty-three varieties of *Agave Azul* 'Weber'. Now, through monoculture, there is only one, a pale-blooded, rather helpless version. Certainly, some will not take to the agenda well. *Karwinskiis*, for example, are notoriously fussy about where they grow. As a producer in Ejutla, Oaxaca told me, 'Some people like to live in the country, and some in the city. That's the way they know how to live and they won't survive any other way.'

Meanwhile, I would suggest enjoying this moment when there is an abundance of truly wild agave mezcals at the *mezcaleria*. They may well become more scarce and more expensive.

Mono-farming is practical for the worker but not for the plant

LAS PLANTAS

Agaves are what make mezcal, mezcal. And it is all the different varieties, and the regions in which they flourish, that make it one of the few spirits that works like a wine.

There are more than two hundred species identified, fifteen of which stand out to me as the main players in production. Identifying them from the car window as you zoom across Mexico is an enormously satisfying pastime. As is identifying them at the *mezcaleria*, decoding local terminology to learn more about what you're sipping and how it came to be there in your *copita*.

¡Salud!

AMERICANA

Name: *Agave americana*
AKA: Serrano; Sierrudo; Americano
Age to maturity: 15–20 years
Height at maturity: 3 metres (10 feet)
Frequency: few **Yield:** high
Leaves: A strange pale green-blue to ghostish white *penca* that cocks outwards two-thirds of the way up.

A formidable plant. Standing next to one in the wild is humbling. A smoky green-blue, it has an unmistakable glow compared with the monochromatic flora about it. This was the plant that inspired Carl Linnaeus to bestow the title of 'agave' on the genus.

Its origins are in the vast North-east of the country, from where, due to the dietary need for its copious sugars, and therefore through an organized distribution, it was extended into the South, where it transformed over time and took the new name of *Agave americana* var. *Oaxacensis*.

Found in
- Guanajuato
- Hidalgo
- Nuevo Leon
- San Luis Potosí
- Tamaulipas

ARROQUEÑO

Name: *Agave americana* var. *Oaxacensis*
AKA: Blanco; Cenizo; Coyote; Sierra Negra
Age to maturity: 20–30 years
Height at maturity: 3 metres (10 feet)
Frequency: limited **Yield:** high
Leaves: Very long, thick and straight with an unmistakable white-ish hue, like the giant apparition of the ghost of *espadín*.

One of the giants of mezcal, growing, towering to a truly formidable size; its *cuioté* shoots to an average of nine metres (thirty feet) and has huge inflorescence, flowers and fruits, to match. Taking as long as it does to reach maturity makes its production as a mezcal relatively limited.

Though it's a great source for other crafts, especially fibre crafts, with the long length of the *pencas* giving a long length of thread. A domesticated variation of the *Agave americana*, created by man and never grown wild. Like some adorable pet monster.

Found in
- Oaxaca
- Puebla

CUPREATA

Name: *Agave cupreata*
AKA: Papalometl; Alto; Tuchi; Papalote
Age to maturity: 10–15 years
Height at maturity: 1 metre (3 feet)
Frequency: abundant **Yield:** medium
Leaves: Wide, brilliant-green spatulas that are often mottled in wild baroque patterns. The leaves are ridged by copper-coloured curvy spines that culminate in a ferocious spike.

The *cupreata* gives soft, floral musks to her mezcals, flavours produced by the romantic setting in which she grows: pine-oak forests, lazy pastures, palm groves and swampy jungle. The indigenous Guerrerans and Michoacános have a deep relationship with her and hold her very dear.

These states have an intensely upheld system of communal and *ejidal* lands in which the *cupreata* grows wild, and how the plant is used is an important matter, taken as a community decision.

Found in
- Guerrero
- Michoacán
- Oaxaca

DURANGENSIS

Name: *Agave durangensis*
AKA: I'Gok; Castilla; Chacaleño; Cenizo
Age to maturity: 15–18 years
Height at maturity: 2 metres (6 feet)
Frequency: plentiful **Yield:** high
Leaves: Grey-green leaves that are wide and thick, concaved and zigzagged.

Endemic to the deserts and pine-oak forest regions that cover the states of Durango and Zacatecas. It tends to give mezcals in the nutty, musty, golden-tobacco-and-leather flavour zone.

There are at least ten variants known to *mezcaleros* in the region of its distribution. Nearly all of which are, at this time, still harvested wild. They flower in the rainy season and group together in the hills.

Unfortunately, as some highlands in the region have been appropriated by narcos, some variants of the *durangensis* are, at this time, impossible to reach.

Found in
• Durango
• Guanajuato
• Zacatecas

ESPADIN

Name: *Agave angustifolia*
AKA: Yavi Incoyo; Doba-yej; Bacanora
Age to maturity: 7–9 years
Height at maturity: 2 metres (6 feet)
Frequency: abundant **Yield:** high
Leaves: Light green meets greyish-blue. Long, neatly distributed and very straight. Not unlike long swords or *espaldas* from which the word *espadin* derives.

Unlike other agaves, at home practically everywhere. For this reason, for the speed at which it reaches maturity, and for its bounty of sugars, it is the work horse of mezcal production, making around 75% of registered mezcals. This leads some to consider *espadin* mezcals a little ho-hum. But their gift for adaptability is what makes them so varied in flavour.

Found in
• Campeche
• Chihuahua
• Durango
• Guerrero
• Jalisco
• Michoacán
• Nayarit
• Oaxaca
• Puebla
• Quintana Roo
• Sonora
• Yucatan
• Zacatecas

INAEQUIDENS

Name: *Agave inaequidens*
AKA: Hocimetl; Lechuguilla
Age to maturity: 15–18 years
Height at maturity: 2.5 metres (8 feet)
Frequency: common **Yield:** high
Leaves: Thick, undulating, light green and yellowish.

A real triffid of an agave. With its teeth growing successively longer and showing more *penca* than *piña*, it appears far more capable of eating a modest-sized human then other species.

But the word *lechuguilla* describes something far more benign; meaning essentially 'frilly', it shares the same etymology as lettuce. This *lechuguilla* – there are two other species that use the name – loves wide open spaces between the pine forests and oak groves of Central Mexico. It's famously used for the production of *pulque*, but also for *raicillas*.

Found in
- Durango
- Jalisco
- Michoacán

JABALI

Name: *Agave convalis*
AKA: Kerchovei; Jabalin
Age to maturity: 8–12 years
Height at maturity: 1.5 metres (5 feet)
Frequency: scarce **Yield:** low
Leaves: A light yellowy-green curving back over its length and edged with red spikes.

A *jabali* is a wild boar and the *jabali* agave gets its name from the way parts of the plant can resemble the attributes of wild boar when they're about to attack.

Its leaves poke up and curl back like the prickly hairs that stick up along a boar's back when it is about to strike, while its giant *cuioté*, rather than opening out like a candelabra, as those of many other agaves do, keeps its seeds all along the fat tip of the stem, looking a little like a 'cat's tail' rush and resembling the formidable horn of a beast in the wild.

Jabali mezcals tend to give light fruit flavours and create an uplifting mood. Highly recommended!

Found in
- Oaxaca

KARWIŃSKII

Name: *Agave karwinskii*
AKA: Bicuixe; Madrecuixe; Tobasiche
Age to maturity: 8–25 years
Height at maturity: 1–2.5 metres (3–8 feet)
Frequency: common **Yield:** low
Leaves: Bordering on tree-like with the agave perched on top of a trunk like a fat spiky green bobble.

Micro-endemic to Oaxaca and the most southern tip of Puebla, due to its being very particular about where it wants to grow. Therefore, few attempts have been made to cultivate them, though they are often grown in rows as a fence. *Karwinskiis* change their height and thickness, as well as the colour, size and shape of their leaves, giving rise to an untraceable number of names. Though, interestingly, in Santiago Matatlán, it is simply known as *cirial* and all the variants are cooked and produced together as one. Tends to give green vegetative flavours and a party vibe.

Found in
- Oaxaca
- Puebla

MAXIMILIANA

Name: *Agave maximiliana*
AKA: Lechuguilla; Tecolote; Valenciana
Age to maturity: 8–15 years
Height at maturity: 1–1.5 metres (3–5 feet)
Frequency: scarce **Yield:** medium
Leaves: Wide and light green with large interspersed dark spines.

The mainstay of *raicilla* production, the *maximiliana* likes the highlands, consolidating the majority of *raicilla* in the Jaliscan mountains west of Tequila. Though their distribution is much wider than the *raicilla* DO, running down the mountain back of the Sierra Madre from Sinaloa to Jalisco and into Durango.

It reproduces only by seed, which is why the plants grow alone as individuals rather than in dense groups. They can also grow to such a size that clusters would be impossible: a full-grown Valenciana is the size of an apple tree.

Found in
- Durango
- Guanajuato
- Jalisco

RHODACANTHA

Name: *Agave rhodacantha*
AKA: Quixe; Chontal; Mezcal; Mexicano
Age to maturity: 20–25 years
Height at maturity: 3.5 metres (12 feet)
Frequency: scarce **Yield:** high
Leaves: Long, straight and fibrous in dark to light green.

Another staggeringly huge agave plant whose *cuioté* reaches an average of nine metres (thirty feet) above the ground. In full bloom, rising from its magnificent three-and-a-half-metre (twelve-foot) dome of leaves, a *mexicano* is a thing to see. At home all the way from Sonora to Oaxaca, she can be found in the foothills at one to two thousand metres (three thousand to seven thousand feet) above sea level, gathering the soils rich in organic material that provide all the nutrients to reach such impressive dimensions.

Found in
- Durango
- Guanajuato
- Guerrero
- Jalisco
- Michoacán
- Nayarit
- Oaxaca
- Puebla
- Sinaloa

SALMIANA

Name: *Agave salmiana*
AKA: Bronco; Cimarrón; Manso; Verde
Age to maturity: 15–20 years
Height at maturity: 2 metres (7 feet)
Frequency: common **Yield:** low
Leaves: Thick and dark green with fat dark spines.

For a time during the nineteenth century, more mezcal was made with this than all other plants. She was also the mother agave, the deity Mayahuel being seen first in her form; she is sometimes still called 'divine'.

Over time, through excessive production and the practice of *capon* (see page 71), the plant began to lose its ability to flower and seed, so now most propagation is done through *hijuelos* (see page 42).

This, along with low yield – four times the weight of *salmiana* is needed to produce the same quantity of mezcal as *espadin* – makes spirits from this typically green and vegetal-flavoured plant hard to find.

Found in
- Coahuila
- Durango
- San Luis Potosí
- Zacatecas

SOTOL

Name: *Dasylirion wheeleri*
AKA: Sotolin; Desert Spoon
Age to maturity: 5–10 years
Height at maturity: 1–1.5 metres (3–5 feet)
Frequency: common **Yield:** medium
Leaves: Grey-green slender blades that fan out to make a brilliant bushy sphere about three feet in diameter.

There are nineteen varieties of the Desert Spoon, sixteen of which are used to make sotol. The plant is related to the lily (as opposed to the agave's asparagus) but the major difference is that sotol, if harvested correctly, *will grow back*. They're also either male or female, the male giving white flowers and the female a pinkish-purple. Agaves are hermaphroditic.

The heart of the cooked plant is eaten and considered one of the power foods for the Rarámari people, famous for their ability to run for hundreds of miles without stopping.

Found in
• Chihuahua
• Coahuila
• Sonora

TEPEZTATE

Name: *Agave marmorata*
AKA: Pitzometl; Curandero
Age to maturity: 12–15 years
Height at maturity: 1.5 metres (5 feet)
Frequency: scarce **Yield:** high
Leaves: Thick, wide army-green leaves with random patterns of pale white-ish green, a little like camouflage.

The *tepeztate* – which I've also rather touchingly heard called the 'ugly duckling' – is a real hot mess laying all sprawled out about the place.

Though for three months during late spring and early summer, at the peak of maturity, her flowers burst into a brilliant crown of bright orange, a uniquely vivacious display within the genus.

This does not escape the eye of the hummingbirds and bats that compete for her nectar, which fosters the vigorous creation of a notable collection of hybrids.

Found in
• Guerrero
• Michoacán
• Oaxaca

TEQUILANA

Name: *Agave tequilana*
AKA: Agave Azul; Agave Blue Weber
Age to maturity: 6–9 years
Height at maturity: 2 metres (6 feet)
Frequency: abundant **Yield:** high
Leaves: Blue-green, long, flat and straight.

I've heard it said that there were once thirty-three variants of this species, internationally famous for its special blue-green hues and as the agave used in tequila. Though industrial farming has tragically made most of these extinct. There is an effort to sustain those that survive and a *tequilana* on offer at a small-batch *mezcaleria* might well be one of those. I highly recommend the experience.

They were singled out for tequila's mass production not only because they hold more sugars than any other species (yielding more mezcal), but also because they tend to be particularly energizing, creating the stimulating high — the tequila buzz — for which tequilas are legendary.

Found in
- Guanajuato
- Jalisco

TOBALÁ

Name: *Agave potatorum*
AKA: Dob-lá; Papalometl; Yauiticushi
Age to maturity: 12–15 years
Height at maturity: 60 centimetres (2 feet)
Frequency: scarce **Yield:** low
Leaves: Tech-like polygon-esque dark green, sometimes almost dark blue, plates for leaves reminiscent of some ancient temple structure.

Papalometl, such a nice word, and meaning the 'butterfly maguey'. Clearly a close cousin of the *cupreata*, they share not only a similar appearance but similar landscape and the same way of reproducing, which is only through seeds and — relying on the bats, birds and bees — pollination.

Typically perfumed and thoroughly prized, due to its small stature the *tobalá* yields precious little mezcal. It would take roughly five times as many of these plants as it would of *espadin* to make the same volume of spirits. Which is why we're likely to see less and less of this, purely wild.

Found in
- Guerrero
- Michoacán
- Oaxaca
- Puebla

THE REGIONAL AGAVE SPIRITS OF MEXICO

'Mezcal is something unique and individual in a world increasingly geared towards mass production and uniformity.' Jesse Estes, barman and agave spirit aficionado

Mexico is anything but uniform. In fact, you might even say that there are many Mexicos. It is a mosaic of cultures and climates, created over long periods of time by the geographically dissected surface of its landscape. While one valley experiences deluge, its neighbours go dry. Cold pine mountain tops form barriers for tropical jungles. Deserts surround the oases. This creates a place of flair and colour, attitude and style. Like mezcal, it is not narrow. It is not predictable. Yesterday I sat to eat a breakfast of *chilaquiles con huevos* when the little old lady next to me pulled out a plastic bag and a square of fried pig skin to share. It's a kind, generous, loose and dangerous place. And it is in this seemingly infinite and varying patchwork that the universe of agave spirits is made.

The character of a people is informed by their environment. Mexico has been informed by its weather patterns, the quality of its soil and its light, by the wildlife and undeniably by its plants, many of which are psychotropic: the mushrooms of the highlands; the Peyote of the deserts (see page 20); and the resplendent agaves that flourish throughout most of the country.

The following pages are a series of sketches about some of the main regions involved in making those agave spirits, whether they are called 'mezcal' or not.

Santiago Matatlán, Oaxaca. Known as the world capital of mezcal

SONORA

CHIHUAHUA

COAHUILA

SINALOA

DURANGO

ZACATECAS

NAYARIT

GUANAJUATO

JALISCO

COLIMA

MICHOACÁN

THE MEZCAL MAP

The wide and wonderful world of mezcal is the story of the ecology and fauna of the enormous land mass of Mexico. Use the cards of Las Plantas (see pages 46–53) to trace where the various agaves thrive and deliver their specific regional mezcals. And get your bearings and sense of place by seeing where they are on this mezcal map.

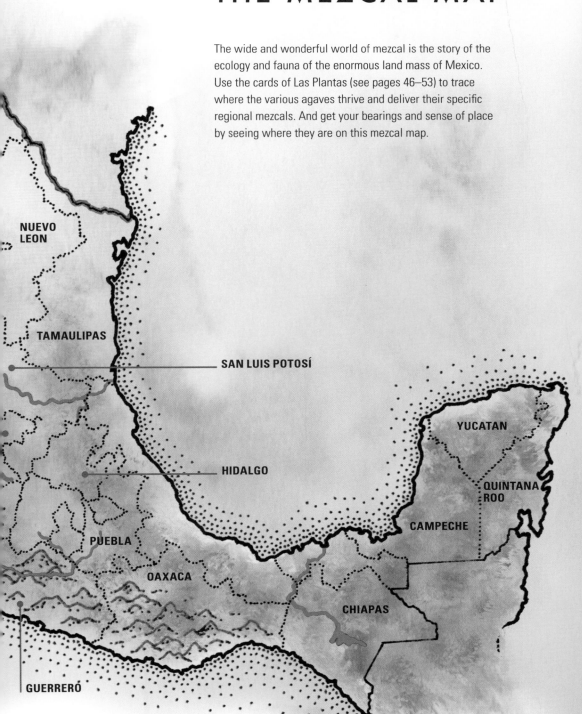

NUEVO LEON

TAMAULIPAS

SAN LUIS POTOSÍ

YUCATAN

HIDALGO

QUINTANA ROO

CAMPECHE

PUEBLA

OAXACA

CHIAPAS

GUERRERO

DURANGO (Central)

Mezcal culture in Durango is old, deep and going strong. It is a vast state north of Central Mexico, which holds the second highest diversity of agaves after Oaxaca.

The state's namesake *Agave durangensis* is in abundance. Most of the mezcals comng out of Durango are wild, as, until recently, there simply hasn't been any demand for cultivation. But that is changing and, increasingly, the state is seen as a promising producer of volume.

Much of production echoes the early industrialization of tequila. Steam ovens are common and some productions still continue in haciendas. In a way, Durangan productions can be seen as snap-shots into Jalisco's past, back to a time when Jalisco still produced with all its available agave varieties. However, the flavours of Durango and the *durangensis* are unmistakably unique: musky tobacco and nut notes are classic and recurring profiles in the state's mezcals.

Many of the wealth of agave variants in Durango have, however, been made inaccessible by the newer industry of narcotics. Organizations involved in drug manufacturing tend, as in other parts of the country, to make their bases in remote highland regions for obvious reasons. Unfortunately for us, this is where many of the agave species like to hang out, too.

Perhaps in time, the growing revitalization of Durango's mezcal production will offer some young men another way forward in life besides gangs, or going north to work in the United States.

GUERRERO (South)

Guerreran *fabriceros* like to remind you that they were making mezcal before the Oaxaqueños. And they're probably right, as mezcal's migration might well have had to pass through Guerrero before reaching today's capital of mezcal.

But Guerrero's mezcals have until very recently – it was illegal to produce there until 1996 – been overlooked. However, as 90% of the state's agave is wild, there is an abundance of fine and traditional mezcals being made.

The *Agave cupreata* is the agave most closely associated with the state. Unlike most other species, it is propagated solely through seed dissemination and pollination. Hummingbirds, night birds, insects and bats drawn by the flowers of the *calehual* – the Nahua word used in Guerrero for the *cuioté* – spread the pollen, giving easy rise to hybrids.

The state is densely wooded and consistently wet. This imparts the characteristic musky, woody, earthy-and-fruity flavours of the mezcals. In Guerrero, a mezcal is only deemed legit if it's at least 50% ABV. That is most likely rooted in the still of the region, a copper and single distillation number: *una refinadora*. What comes off the still is called *refino*.

Other local practices include a remarkably long *capon* period of five years (see page 71). The first time *capon* was explained to me was through the mind-blowing experience of my first Guerreran mezcal, a Sanzekan production by Maestro Tomas. I'll never forget it. That is the power and joy of pure mezcals: they're unforgettable. Guerrero is home to many.

JALISCO / RAICILLA (South-west)

In a culture with as much legend and lore as that of mezcal, to be the most legendary of the lot takes some doing.

I first heard of *raicilla* from a gifted albino Swedish vogue champion (the dance, not the magazine). She insisted that it wasn't like others, that it had a magical quality, and she was hard to doubt.

At the time, 2009, it was not easy to find. Apart from a handful of *mezcalerias* in Mexico, the only place to find the stuff was in remote pockets of Jalisco. Now – miraculously – we find it in Europe, the United States and elsewhere. It's begun to step out of the realm of myth. Completely.

Raicilla is about to receive its own Denomination of Origin. For better or worse. All *raicillas* will now *have* to be made in Jalisco. The oven will have to be above ground. And all the plants harvested within the state.

Raicilla exists in the shadow of its giant neighbour, tequila; the state isn't big enough for both of them… or at least the most choice lands aren't. So *raicillas* are made in the nooks and crannies of the highlands, far from major towns.

This has limited *raicilla*'s growth but, arguably, has preserved the culture and phenomenally good mezcals. Could it also have led to the legendary reputation of an especially magical mezcal? Was it just that all *raicillas* are hand-crafted? Or could it have been the plants?

One of the agaves used in production is called the Valenciana. It's an ample, sprawling creature, that can grow to an immense size: three metres (ten feet) both tall and wide, with a bulb weighing eighty kilos (one hundred and seventy-six pounds). A whopper. The longer plants grow, the more experience they develop of how to maximize their potential. It could be from this that some of the magic arrives.

Raicilla has had a long time to incubate. As it emerges into the world, the DO parameters set will, we hope, further protect its famed quality, and keep the legend alive.

MICHOACÁN (South)

Some of the earliest forms of production are still practised here: the use of rock-pit or clay-pot fermentation tanks, and the burying of bottled mezcals in the earth to 'rest'. Where other areas found themselves close to markets, Michoacáno mezcal remained isolated. Until recently, it remained solely for the community, its fiestas and ceremonies.

The state is wooded, thick with old forests of oak and pine. It looks like southern Scotland in July, but all year round. There's a lot of rainfall and a lot of sun. The *Agave cupreata* has a very distinctive taste. There's a fruity and earthy musk about it and something floral, no doubt due to this unique environment. The distinctive flavours are pronounced by how few producers there are, making the mezcals especially regional.

The ceremonial view is still strong here; it has escaped much of the modernity of the North. 'Closer to the border and further from God,' as my friend Hector explains. The making of mezcal includes a *curandera* blessing of the agaves, sprinkling them with a branch soaked in mezcal before they're placed on the hot coals. And mezcals are buried, significantly, for an incubation period of nine months before being delivered into the light of day.

Some of these practices are a long way away from how many elsewhere work today. But the producers and their communities are fighting to become part of the international scene. They feel they've been left out of the action for too long. Indeed, when the DO was formed, Michoacán was one of the states left off the billing. Though *vinterias*, as they're called here, were producing, it was illegal to do so, and the remarkable abundance of – to us – priceless *cupreata*, was harvested wild and simply sold as fodder for the agave syrup market in the United States.

An agonizing fact for those of us who have experienced the exceptional mezcals of Michoacán.

OAXACA (South)

Oaxaca is a special place. A cultural nexus. Formal, lively, proud and flowing to its own wavelengths, it is a country within the country and home to several nations (and sixteen languages) within that. A constellation of communities revolving around a series of marketplaces where the people of surrounding townships bring their crafts for trade. One of these crafts is mezcal.

Geographically and ecologically, Oaxaca is the most diverse place in Mexico. Desert, lush jungle, cool cloudy pine forest and coastline. These dramatically varied environments create the broadest range of agaves on Earth. And out of them, its peoples create the wide, celebrated range of mezcals.

Around 80% of the world's mezcal comes from Oaxaca, and Santiago Matatlán, the self-proclaimed *capital mundial de mezcal*, produces its fair share of those. The small town of the central valley floor has a whopping eighty registered *palenques* with a population of only three thousand souls.

There are more craft and clay-pot distilled mezcals here than in other states, which adds to the diversity. But what is internationally known as the classic mezcal flavour: rich, oily cooked agave and pepper notes, with a high ABV, is pure Oaxaca.

What really makes Oaxaca sing is the strength of its regional cultures, each with their own way to make mezcal, fabrics and food, pottery and painting, dances… and music.

Oaxaca is famous for is fiestas. These spark up in my neighbourhood at all hours of the day and night. Out of nowhere, *bandas*, accompanied by the bomb-like blasts of fireworks that shake the windows, trigger car alarms and rain down debris for a full half-minute afterwards. This morning it was 6am. It could be 10am or 2am. Often it's both. A savaging from a lightning-fast brass band is never far away. Tubas, trumpets, slide trombones. A drummer or two. They literally shred. Tear through melodies. It makes your hair stand on end. In Oaxaca, a village without a band is seen as slightly bereft. Like a village without a pub. For hours without stopping, the band never repeats a tune. Everyone comes out and drifts along with them through the streets. Mezcal is administered unsparingly to all.

PUEBLA (South-central)

'It's weird.' Jason Cox of 5 Sentidos (see page 138) was filling me in on all things Poblano. Though the region where production is concentrated is relatively small — one hundred square kilometres (thirty-nine square miles) — almost every type of mezcal process is being employed here.

Wood, clay, copper, steel and oil-barrel stills, as well as an interesting number the Poblanos call the 'French still', which is made of four copper plates, each growing wider as it descends, reminiscent of an ornate fountain of the Tuileries. Then there's the fermentation: plastic, animal hide, wood, clay, rock pits…

What is also strange is how little awareness there is about it all. Puebla is a large and switched-on cosmopolitan city. At present, most people there think their mezcals are all coming out of Oaxaca; they have no idea that, in fact, they're being made only an hour away down the road. Even many of the producers seem unaware of others nearby.

This is probably because Puebla has only just been accepted into the mezcal DO. Also because, I've heard, a lot of mezcals produced in Puebla are bought up and shipped to Oaxaca to be added to the blends of mezcal companies needing to make volume to fulfil demand (see page 90 for more on blends).

Puebla is an obvious choice for this lamentable situation. The state is close to Oaxaca and has a ton of great agaves, especially *tobalá*, *tepaztate*, *espadin* and *cupreata*.

Perhaps, as Puebla becomes more well known for its eclectic mezcals, it will use more of its own agaves and we'll taste more of the land. Jason bottles a number of these Poblano mezcals with 5 Sentidos and they're cracking.

SONORA / BACANORA (North)

Bacanora has everything going for it. A great name — even if it does sound a little like a dance only done at weddings — a legendary reputation, and now its own Denomination of Origin. For the Sonorãnos, it's about time.

In a near-deserted region of the North, using *Agave pacifica*, this often-delicious mezcal has been made for centuries. Though for all of us living outside the state, it's not something you hear a great deal about.

Yet a *bacanora* is often a safe punt. The logic for this lies with the theory of the underdog. Tequilas are everywhere. Mezcal is hot and new. But *bacanora*… the wedding jam? Whoever's behind it has to believe in it.

Having said that… last night I had the maddest mezcal I have ever encountered and it was a *bacanora*. This tasted like an erratic, kitsch, interpretative dance done in a downstairs bathroom by a batty grandmother scattering dried herbs. And that was just on the nose. To say it was flamboyant would be to suggest it was capable of composure. It was that mad.

I did finish it, however, because, underneath, it was a true expression of whatever the hell was going on in that pocket of Sonora in that particular moment. Mezcals… you never can tell what's going to come at you next.

CELEBRATE
GATHER
GROW
POUR
CRAFT
LIVE

JALISCO / TEQUILA (South-west)

There are those who drink tequila and those who drink mezcal and, it must be said, that it looks a lot like never the twain shall meet. But a finely made tequila is a wonderful thing. The accuracy and sheer delicacy of the flavours make them rightfully coveted.

Some of these are produced by the new school, whose focus on terroir is inspired by vintners, and creates memorable vintages. Part of their success has come from reintroducing techniques such as the stone ovens or *tahonas* of the past.

But these pioneers are a drop in the giant sea of big business. Most tequila is manufactured on a massive scale in factories where, if it were not for the mountains of agave and the overwhelming smell of fermenting *mosto*, you'd be hard-pushed to know what was being made.

Though, to be honest, I did find my visits thrilling. The chrome, the dials. Ladders, tanks and pipes, several storeys tall. Climbing about on the grilled cross-walks, you can lose judgement of what is up and what is down. These are the places that 007 seemed to find himself in vintage Bond, having penetrated the inner lair of some mad mastermind, where he is forced to punch it out with hordes of baddies wearing matching clobber (outfits).

Today, these methods seem weirdly dated. But tequila, industrial or craft, is part of a very deep, rich and strong culture – out of all the agave spirits it is the one with the strongest identity – and people are bound to it, economically, culturally and emotionally.

And for that it remains valuable.

For many of those devotees, the hybrid *tabernas* that harness the best of the industrial power and combine it with a modern mindfulness of responsible farming and craft production techniques are cause for celebration.

ZACATECAS (Central)

It's not easy to find Zacatecan mezcals. Which is, at first glance, surprising, as in the nineteenth century it was one of the states producing the highest volume of mezcal in the country. It had a huge market demand from the workforce of the mines – heavily exploited under conditions that would make anyone thirsty – from the second half of the sixteenth century onward, just as mezcal began to emerge.

Furthermore, Zacatecas boasts an abundance of agaves: *salmiana*, *americana* and *durangensis*, but now production is limited to modern industrial units, with a tiny scattering of craft *fabricas*. These reflect the style of the nineteenth-century heyday: *mamposterias*, column stills, copper and steel, often set in hacienda locations.

I've yet to try one, but I met someone who had. An anthropology researcher from University College London, based in Jalisco. She'd spotted a sign by the freeway that runs out to San Luis Potosí and given it a go. She'd passed the sign a number of times and one day decided to brave it.

Apparently she pulled up and, having previously visited roadside *fabricas*, she could tell this did not seem like the others. Extremely chaotic, part dump-site, men staggering about, who appeared to be under the influence of more than just the hooch. She decided to buy rather than try, took three bottles and – smiling and smiling and retreating back to her car – she took off. Told me they were the nicest mezcals she's ever tasted.

SPECIALITIES

PECHUGA

Pechugas are mezcals distilled three times, with natural materials added for flavouring in the third distillation. Typically fruits and meats (*pechuga* means 'breast', as in turkey), though, to be honest, anything will do. I heard of a chap in Puebla who would make *pechuga* from whatever you brought him: lizards, your mum's *molé* recipe…

But I'm not a fan. A great mezcal already has plenty going on. With all the extra flavours it can get a bit much. Though that's not always the point. Known sometimes as celebration mezcals, they are for special occasions, which suits their extravagant flavour.

Pechugas are a product of the impulse to experiment, as every great *mezcalero* does. And it is a way of further introducing the *palenques*' terroir, as the flavourings are what's growing in – or running around – the back yard.

SOTOL

Sotol is achieving the recognition of mezcal and tequila. Though a kindred spirit, the plant is not an agave, and the drink not officially a mezcal.

Before the Spanish conquistadors came, Mexico was two lands. The North was harsh and arid; the people nomadic. Central to their diet was sotol, the 'desert spoon'. (The base of a stem may be eaten like an artichoke leaf. The remnant ['quid'] resembles a spoon and can be used as one. Sites have been found full of quids thousands of years old.)

Each plant takes fifteen years to mature and yields only one bottle of sotol. The core is cooked, fermented and distilled.

Rock paintings along the Rio Grande depict Sotol as a spiky-haired goddess, and traces of a mild beer-like brew from the plant are dated at 8,000 BC. When the Spanish pushed North in the sixteenth century, they brought stills, and sotol began to be made.

During the following centuries, sotol weathered the same taxes and prohibitions as mezcal. But, during US Prohibition, mobsters in Chicago approached *sotoleros* as potential bootleggers. Sotol, however, was deemed too expensive (some people will never get it), so the ever-wise guys asked them to make whiskey. Some complied… others hid in the mountains. One such was Don Cuco. Sotol, the spirit, and the practices for making it, stem from the knowledge of this one man.

In 1976, the Mexican government granted licences to the sons of Don Cuco to make sotol. The way Don Cuco had taught his boys how to cut, cook, distil and adjust – the gospel of sotol – is how it is still done today.

PEOPLE, PROCESS, PRODUCTION

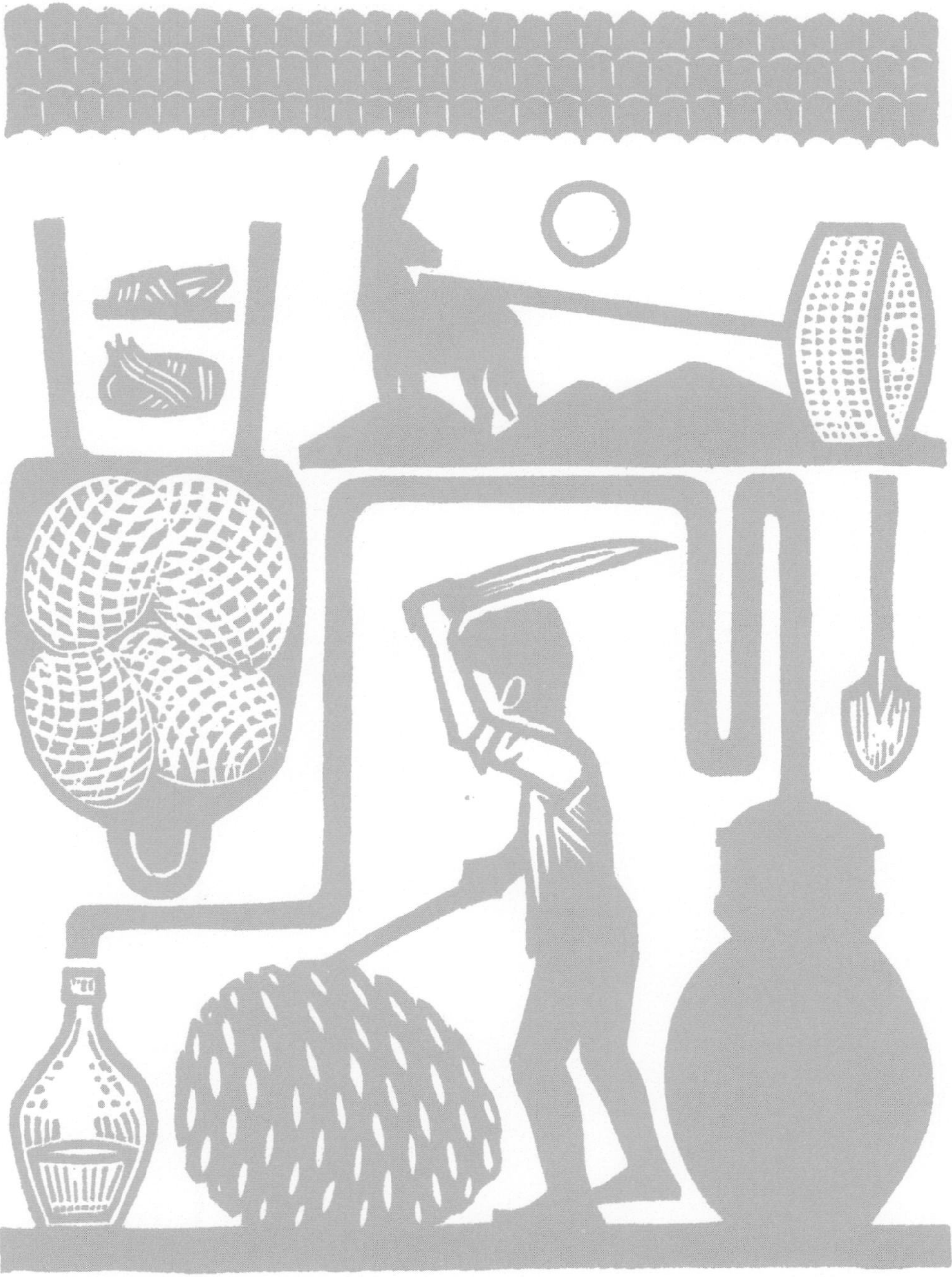

HARVEST
ROAST
CRUSH
FERMENT
DISTIL
TASTE

THE PROCESS

The beautiful thing about mezcal is how creative it is. A thousand choices and actions, some big, many microscopic, take place differently each time a *maestro* fires up the oven and makes a new batch. It's improvisation made in response to all the circumstances at hand.

It's also incredibly hard work. Rewarding — everyone I asked said it made them feel good to do it — but proper hard, nonetheless. The work day commences at the first crack of dawn and continues until the job is done. During distillation this might be non-stop for seventy-two hours.

In the world of mezcal, time takes on new meaning. On average, a *silvestre* takes fifteen years to mature. If a batch calls for one hundred and fifty of them, that's more than two thousand years of growth in the oven. Agaves a *mezcalero* planted, he'll have to wait many years to taste. The older ones know they'll never enjoy the fruits of their labours.

For us to taste fine mezcals demands that a *mezcalero* forfeit the luxury of industry. In industrial mezcal, 'cooking' is done at the push of a button. In traditional mezcal, not only does it take five men all day to build the *tapada* — the oven — but it might take five days and nights for the agave to cook. Sometimes more. This scale of hard graft is important to grasp. For one, it explains the price. More importantly, it suggests the cultural context in which they're made.

Mezcal is rural by nature. It began life by a river, near plenty of wood, surrounded by wild agaves: the essential ingredients. The way the communities and families that make it live are often quite unfamiliar to most of us sipping a splash in our modern cities today. We need to reset our perceptions to fully grasp the joy of mezcal. The best way to do this is to visit Oaxaca. Or Michoacán, or Guerrero. Or you can simply listen carefully to what your soul tells you about work and time and the elements when you're sipping proper pure *mezcales*.

THE HARVEST

Unlike most other crops grown to make alcohol, the agave takes many years to mature and is a one-time-only deal; it's culled at harvest. Other plants revolve around an annual harvest — grapes, for instance — or are constantly in season, such as sugar cane. But agaves mature at different rates and need to be selected for harvest. An *agavero* will know his crops individually.

I heard a lovely story once about a man who had lived next to a colossal *Arroqueño* all his life. It was forty-five years old when he finally decided it was time for it to be harvested. The harvesting of agaves is millennia old and was accompanied by rituals: songs, prayers, offerings to Mayahuel. Few practise these today, but it's easy to imagine that this *mezcalero*, at least, had a quiet moment before he brought his old neighbour, the *Arroqueño*, down.

Row of cuiotés

However mindful one may be during the task, it must be done well. It takes fresh plants to make good mezcal and the leaves need to be trimmed close to the core to avoid bitterness from the leaf stem. How does one harvest a fifty-kilo (one hundred and ten pound), two-metre (six-foot) plant, bristling with barbed arms, exactly? This is the duty of the *cortador* (cutter) and it needs to be done in less than ten minutes. Demanding, highly skilled work.

It's also vital that it is not done too soon. Agaves have a central stem called the *cuioté*. At the peak of maturity it begins to shoot and push its great phallic stalk-like appendage up through the rosette of its leaves, out into the sky to flower and seed. It's the climax of its long life and in that moment it gives everything it's got, all its energy, sap and sugars to the task. Mercilessly, for optimum flavour, the *campesino* must cut the *cuioté* mid-growth to harness the peak of that power. The stunned, neutered agave, or *capon*, stands rooted to the earth for months as it blindly pumps more sugar into its wounded heart until, finally, it expires.

Ruthless, certainly. But it is mandatory to attain the best results and, thus, the tradition. However, with increasing demand for mezcal, the practice of *capon* is now often the exception, and clearly labelled on the bottle as a selling point when it *is* done. That extra year that the plant is left in the ground is a long time for industry to wait. More and more, farmers harvest agaves younger and younger, making for fewer sugars in the plant and less structure in its fibres, causing issues that have to be accounted for later in the process. Changes, changes.

A cortador *prepares* piñas *in Oaxaca*

Maestro *in his garden in San Andres, Oaxaca*

TERROIR

In mezcal, the variations of production, and thus of the product itself, are myriad. Traditional techniques change from village to village and region to region across the country. There are parameters, of course – the agave must be cooked, the mash fermented and ultimately distilled – but within that, anything is possible.

There are two factors, however, that determine the outcome of a batch above all. One is the hand of the producer, *la mano*. '*Tiene buena mano*' is a way of saying that someone has that certain touch, a gift. To make truly wonderful mezcal, the *mezcalero* must have this. They must also be working with the natural surroundings, the terroir.

~

More and more it is being understood that the location of plant growth and production was, all along, the defining factor. During the mounting excitement of the past few years, a lot of mezcal brands have placed emphasis on the variety of agave used. Naturally, this is important and fascinating. But a *tobalá* made in Ejutla might well taste unrecognizable to a *tobalá* distilled thirty miles away in Chichicapam.

Meanwhile, two different species of agave at the same *palenque* will share a common structure of flavours: a subtle theme; a sense of place. It is terroir: the soil and its altitude, its water and fauna, that is the way to understand our mezcals. And the variables are considerable across a landscape so large: parched valley floors, cloudy pine forests, humid jungle, pasture and coastline.

The agaves, especially, considering the length of time they take to grow, like grapes, for example, absorb these factors and reflect them when used to make drinks. But the location of a *palenque* within the landscape further sharpens the individuality of the distillate, and is in on the flavouring process. It's like a sponge of flavour and the master *mezcalero* is intuitively aware of how to manipulate that.

The wood used in the fire, gathered locally; the water used in fermentation, its mineral content; the fauna, after all those years soaking up both the sunshine and the moonlight… everything in traditional production allows these unique, natural, site-specific phenomena to express themselves as the flavours in your mezcal. But none more so than the yeast.

~

The sum total of all these elements, this whirl of natural phenomena, orchestrated by *la mano*, is why we continue to return to the bar to sample, contemplate and learn about mezcal. Mapping the terroir. Tasting the land. Each pearly drop the concentration, the very essence of its natural surroundings. Nature distilled.

A Filipino still, Jalisco

THE PALENQUE

The root meaning of the word *palenque* means 'clearing'. In Oaxaca, clandestine operations began to be known as *palenques* when, after years of prohibitions, productions became hidden away. Up in the hills, in the woods and valleys. If there was water, wood and agaves, anywhere would suit mezcal just fine. In fact, the more immersed in nature, the more the flavours of a mezcal would meet their full potential.

To this day, traditional mezcal distilleries – *palenques* in Oaxaca, *vinterias* in Michoacán, *fabricas* in Guerrero or *tabernas* in Jalisco – are almost entirely open-air affairs with, typically, a *palapas* shelter for the fermentation tanks and the stills. More often than not, they are extremely rustic: dirt floor, structures fashioned from the natural materials growing at hand. At first glance, one wonders how on Earth a set-up like that can make something as exquisite as mezcal. That these entirely rustic, if not primitive, distilleries can produce arguably the most sophisticated spirit in the world is yet another delightful paradox of mezcal.

HORNO – THE OVEN

The practice, millennia old, of roasting agave over hot coals buried under the earth, is the first step towards making mezcal. During the roast, the agave is converted from bitter, caustic vegetation to sweet, soft, caramelized food. Cooking one or two plants to feed the tribe would take some know-how. Cooking six tonnes (seven tons) of it, evenly, over five or six days, in a three-metre (ten-foot) deep pit, five metres (fifteen feet) across, buried out of sight with mats and earth, using nothing even as technical as a thermometer, might, I dare say, take mastery.

The palenque

Madrecuishe *and* espadin *ready to go on the hot rocks*

The tapada *before being covered and sealed*

Watching *maestro* prepare the *tapada* (from *tapar*, 'to cover') is to witness the artist at work. A multitude of considerations, observations, projections and calculations to some long-developed, hard-won metric are all at play as he circles the oven. Where which woods will stand or lay. Lay under which stones, and when said stones are to be added. Which plants will be placed on which stones, and when. The different sizes of them all. The type of agave they are. Their maturity. Decisions that matter and are carefully being made at all times, while there is no time at all to waste! Overcooked agaves give a burnt flavour. Undercooked — there's no popping it all back in for another wee bit — means you'll be short of sugars. It's tricky to get it all just so.

And the sum of this whirr of decisions is all unfolding *once the flames are lit*. The only thing the *maestro* has at initiation is the wood stacked on the pit floor. Construction of a *tapada* is made *while it is on fire!* It takes all day to build. It gets very hot. It is thirsty work.

~

I heard a nice story, once. There was a road being laid out not far from a *palenque*, the first road to be paved in that remote stretch of the country. It occurred to the *maestro* that the pile of tarmacadam sitting by the roadside would burn nicely, slowly, in the heart of the *tapada*. So, a team went down and chucked a healthy load into the back of the truck, brought it to the *palenque* and put it to use. Apparently, the mezcal was great; all these diesel-y notes. This is the creativity of the *maestro*. Not to mention how the world turns out there some days in the deep cut of the mezcal trails.

LA MOLINA – THE CRUSH

Some say that the way you crush cooked agave makes no difference to the flavour. Others are adamant that it does. Recently, the Mexican government offered subsidies to registered *palenques* that included terrifically powerful, handsome, green, spanking-new wood-chippers for making mash. Many *mezcaleros* took to it without question, as crushing cooked agave is some of the more back-breaking work that must needs be done around the *palenque*. Others refused the offer outright. At Alipús, a craft mezcal distillery, they conducted an experiment.

Each of their *maestros* made two batches — one crushed with their usual techniques, one with the wood-chipper — making sure every step except for the crushing was carried out just the same. They gathered and tasted the results to decide which they preferred. Not one of them chose a mezcal from the wood-chipper. The traditions develop for a reason.

Some villages crush their mash by hand by swinging the least aerodynamic wooden hammer you can imagine, or simply by dropping a club straight down on the cooked agave as it sits in the *canua*, a dug-out log resembling — yes — a canoe. Some use a huge stone wheel — the *tahona* — pulled by mule, or the aforesaid green chopper. Either way, it's got to be done to prepare the mash for fermentation.

FERMENTATION

For some, this is a subject of unequalled fascination; the results a nutritional cure-all and the process a daily way of life. For others, it can be a bit off-putting, so, for the benefit of the latter, I'll try to keep it simple.

Every organic material, once living, left to rot, will ferment. Creation: destruction. The laws of life itself are at the heart of fermentation. Wild yeasts, through digestion, give us, on the one hand, carbon monoxide and, on the other, alcohol.

It's a bit foul when you pay too close attention, so we'll leave it at that. Happily, good things come from it… importantly, *tepache*, which is the result of fermenting cooked agave. *Tepache* is ancient, full of nutrients and healthy microbes. At around three or four ABV, it is mild alcohol that people have been drinking for thousands of years. When distilled, it makes mezcal.

As with each of the other stages in the production process, the choices made during the fermentation process matter. The length of time it is allowed to run is key and varies with the weather due to temperature, and with which plant is used in the cooking. A *madrecuishe*, for example, which contains fewer sugars than the very sweet *espadin*, will need to ferment for longer to reach the levels of alcohol necessary for distillation.

Other decisions surround the instigation of fermentation. Unlike most other spirit manufacturing, traditional mezcal does not use a processed yeast. The yeasts, microbial creatures living all about us on surfaces and in the atmosphere, feast on the sugars of the decomposing agave. But this ambient yeast can, particularly in cold weather, need a jump-start. There are ways of doing this naturally. Water helps – the chopped, cooked agave sits in water in vats – but other natural materials can be added. Adding *pulque* (fermented un-cooked agave sap, see page 22) is a nice touch. Its high sugar content gets things going and it can add a moist chalky flavour to the final mezcal.

Some argue that the vats used to hold the mash don't have any influence on the flavours of the mezcal. That you can use anything you like – plastic, steel, wood or clay – and that it's just a container for the *tepache*. But I tend to think that they do. The most common, *tiñas* as they are sometimes called, are shoulder-high barrels similar to those used in wine making. And they develop flavours of their own over time and are the home of living yeasts that are invaluable.

Either way, the different practices – even if only on a cultural level, helping to seal the regional bond – are important. Rock pit tanks are a tradition in Michoacán, for example. A practice that was especially useful during the prohibition years, being the best way to keep your mash safely hidden from sight while it ferments.

Morbid side-story here: it's suggested, and it does make sense, that the practice began with the use of burial tombs that lay in the rocks, already carved, for ancient funereal services. To some, equally morbid would be the use of animal hide, stretched over a bamboo frame. Another significant tradition.

Fermentation tiñas *in Zoquitlán, Oaxaca.*

DISTILLATION

Distillation, at the end of the day, is the quantum leap, the crucial difference between the ancient fermented drinks of *pulque* or *tepache* (see pages 22 and 80) and mezcal. It is the main event of the whole process.

The origins of distillation lie in the Middle East and its roots in the art of the alchemist, whose goal was to extract the living essence of the natural world around him. This was done using the four principal elements, as they were called: Earth, Water, Air and Fire. To many people, this is, with all its spiritual and symbolic implications, just exactly what *mezcaleros* are doing today.

The idea of extracting a pure essence through the evaporation and recapturing of a spirit – now purer, whiter, reborn – in a condensation, was the thinking behind the still's development in the first place. And the arabesque apparatus used to make mezcal in *palenques* today – the copper pot still – has changed little since then. The ancient alchemists would certainly recognize what the *mezcaleros* were up to.

The pot, which is the top of the apparatus, is placed over the bottom pan that sits above a heat source, sealed (in Mexico, using, among other things, damp tortillas), with the fermented mash inside. As the mash heats, its alcohols evaporate, rise and are cooled by an external water source to create condensation droplets that are caught and collected within the still.

Do this twice with *tepache*... and you have mezcal. The type of pot still you use – the material it's made from, the shape and size – is often dictated by the traditions of where you live and work. There are four main types.

THE ALEMBIC

Copper, Middle Eastern in origin and two thousand years old. The design is extremely simple and credited to a Maria Judea of the first century CE. It gets its name from *al-ambiq*, the Arabic translation of a Greek apparatus, the *ambix*, meaning 'double-barrelled'. It's the classic pot still and the one we see most at the *palenques*. Typically, you would need to distil twice with an alembic to reach a strong enough spirit to work with.

THE REFRESCADOR

Also typically copper, but with a different inner system from the alembic. It is structured in such a way as to carry out two distillations within the one pass, so the mezcal doesn't have to leave the still until it has reached the fullness of its potential strength. An explanation given to me by Joel Hernández, of Casa Cortes (see page 139), equated the process to serving a dish of food straight from the oven. He pointed out that food that's cooked and then reheated was rarely as tasty. Hard to argue with that and there was absolutely no arguing with the phenomenally delicious quality of his and his father's distillates.

The simple workings of the Filipino still

CLAY-POT STILLS

Mezcals distilled using these stills are some of the most sought after and coveted craft spirits in the world. The still itself could not be less glamorous: essentially they look like an upside-down flower pot with a bamboo shoot poking out the side. They are sealed with *bagasso* – the pulpy fibres left after mashing the agaves – and in their interiors hang the tip of an agave leaf to catch condensation. This rudimentary set-up delivers mesmerizingly deep and sensual mezcals. However, as you might imagine, the stills are also fantastically inefficient, hence the scarcity of clay-pot mezcals and their correspondingly high price.

THE FILIPINO STILL

This could not be more simple or effective. A hollowed-out tree trunk, two pans and a hole in the ground. Why complicate anything? Quite possibly, paradoxically, the more primitive the set-up, the tastier the results. The art of great mezcal seems to be not in bending nature to one's will, but working with it to allow for the most direct communication of its essence and flavours.

COMPOSITION

The creative process of making mezcal begins in the soil, years before the oven is lit. Every stage from then on offers a chance to influence the outcome. No step is more important than another, yet certainly the final rung of the ladder takes on a special import: composition.

This is the process of separating the mezcal into different batches according to the alcohol strength and type as it comes off the still. From here, the *mezcalero* recombines the spirit to create the best balance for that batch. Decisions here are irreversible; you can't press 'undo'. But it is a process undertaken alone. The approach used is personal, often inherited like a recipe, and took years to perfect, so tends to be a well-guarded secret.

~

It is the Bermuda Triangle of the process and rarely explained. On the occasions that I've pried and brought the subject up, I've been headed off with only the most basic outlines, a nervous chuckle, a shrug and, from one *mezcalero*, a poetic description of himself and the moon.

Which is all very well, but, troublingly, composition is one of the blind spots for COMERCAM as well. Any rules about how the spirit is 'brought to measure' are vague and allow lots of wiggle room for shoddy takes on the traditional. Batches can be collected from different producers – making it hard to regulate the quality – and then mixed into a soup to be labelled 'artisanal' (see page 33). These mezcals are then sent off around the world (they'd be unacceptable locally), with the budding *mezcalero* abroad unaware they're being short-changed. Fortunately, some brands, like Vago (see page 180), are fastidiously traditional while keeping an open policy on every stage of their production. I got to witness their *maestro*, Aquilano, at work one day, helping a friend bring his mezcal to strength.

We were in Zoquitlán, Oaxaca, when there was mention of a visit to the adjacent valley, where another *mezcalero* had been making fine mezcals but – new to COMERCAM and its restrictions – needed a hand bringing a batch to measure. We hopped in the truck and drove up a madly rugged road, on to a wide *mesa* full of long grasses, where – dreamlike – thirty or forty indigenous men, women and children sat by the side of the track. We stopped to share mezcal with them, then trundled down into the next-door ravine and pulled up to a *palenque* built into the ruins of a crumbling hacienda. Here, the *maestros* went to work, bringing the spirit home.

The two had concocted a mix of *colas y aqua* (see page 88) which was allowed to sit for three weeks before being used as a diluting solution. The mezcal stood at 60.5% where things tasted fine, though it was certainly a bit stiff and the flavours were boxy. Through calculating the volume we had in litres and the current ABV, we could add the precise amount of solution needed to bring the spirit to the next level for tasting. This brought it down to 56.5%. We tasted and added, tasted and added, until we reached 51.2% ABV where it opened out in a new way, giving a depth and scope that wasn't there before. It was clear to all that the potential of that mezcal had been unlocked.

Don Benigno, of the Sanzekan cooperative, Guerrero

Mezcal for sale, Oaxaca

Measuring the ABV with the venencia *and* jicara

THE VENENCIA – MAKING THE GRADE

Making mezcal is a creative endeavour, but it is also technical work, particularly in these final stages of production when the distillate, now off the still, needs to be divided into sections corresponding to the different types of alcohol it is made from.

This is traditionally done with the *venencia*, a thirty centimetre (foot-long) bamboo shoot used like a straw to draw up the mezcal, from where it is released again into a *jicara* – a gourd cup – to count the bubbles, or *perlas*. The size of *las perlas*, the amount of them and how long they last indicate – to a 0.5th percentage point of accuracy – the ABV, or *el grado*. Accuracy is crucial, as different parts of the distillate carry different types of alcohol which, in turn, carry different properties – some good, some not so good – and different flavours.

It's a perilous moment. The slightest mistake could spell disaster. The parameters of COMERCAM are tight and can be tricky to limbo beneath, especially in regards to the amounts of acidity and methanol present, two areas that carry a lot of flavour. If these levels are too high, it will render the spirit unsaleable in the realm of Denomination of Origin, waste weeks of work and significant investment into precious plants.

~

There are traditions and habits that influence how a *mezcalero* approaches grading. Experience handed down and gathered over time. How that experience is applied and what decisions are made are paramount. They are also final. They directly impact the final outcome. They *are* the final outcome. Using the *venencia*, the *mezcalero* separates the distillate into three parts:

Las perlas

The Heads, or *Puntas*

These come off the still first. They lie somewhere between 65 and 80% ABV and carry a lot of flavour. There is a culture of drinking the heads. Mostly by the older fellows, myself included. It's good for drinking after a hard day. And for setting fire to things around the yard.

The Tails, or *Colas*

These come last, carry the lowest ABV and bear mostly bitter flavours.

The Body or Heart, or *Cuerpo o Corazon*

The main event, the majority of your distillate, this lies between 28 and 65% ABV. It's this that is brought to measure, that is balanced.

REPOSADOS

The practice of ageing spirits is an old one. In tequila culture these are *reposados* and *añejos*, 'rested' in barrels. Depending on the barrels, old or new, which woods and what-have-you, you get different flavours. In mezcal, this is a new habit... and it can provoke charged responses.

For purists, there are two lines of thinking: one, that it's a shame; two, that you shouldn't do it. Craft mezcals come off the still already expressing their complexities. When they are put in barrels, that identity is lost to the flavours in the wood.

~

Tequila, in the late nineteenth century, set its sights on American markets and makers imitated bourbon, whiskey and rum by resting their spirits in barrels. These *reposados* proved appealing to the Mexican market as well, especially in those parts where a romance for the Old World was strongest. It did look a little like brandy, after all.

As tequila became industrial during the twentieth century and began to lose flavour through modern processes, *reposados* became essential. But it's not all cynical. Many *mezcaleros* do choose to rest craft mezcals in wood, through an urge to experiment, often with incredible results. *Reposados* have a different effect on the drinker as well. They're more soothing than their *joven* (young) counterparts, a by-product of tannins in the wood.

~

A tradition in resting as old as mezcal itself, however, is that of burying mezcal in glass flagons (*garrafónes*), to gather itself. The DO sets the minimum time at twelve months, undermining the evocative tradition of a nine-month incubation. However long it's left, nothing is meant to come of it. The bottle is sealed. But the effect, if you try one, is extremely pronounced. The spirit seems to thicken. Like many of the better things in life, this is inexplicable.

The sacred and the profane, Arandas, Jalisco

THE GOOD, THE BAD AND THE UGLY

MEZCALES CONEJOS

Mezcal has often faced adversity. And today brings fresh problems. Narcos commandeering agave-rich highlands and mezcal-producing villages. Unsustainable pressure on cultivated agave; diminishing numbers of *silvestres* and rare varieties. Deforestation for firewood and poisoning of streams and rivers. What next? Well, ironically, it is certain well-meaning brands that pose probably the biggest threat to mezcal's survival as a culture.

Mezcal has always appealed to people with a creative bent. And in recent times it has become *de rigeur* – as a hip urbanite worth one's salt – to get involved. This has led to a boom in mezcal brands (in 2015, more than one hundred new brands were registered in Mexico City alone), many of which have not been well-thought-out. Some, whose beautifully conceived presentation and advertising campaigns have generated far more sales than their *palenques* can provide for, are faced with difficult decisions.

For these brands, the only way to fulfil their business demands is to make changes in production. Though their intentions may well have been honourable at first – we all fall in love with mezcal – when faced with the choice of prestige and financial success, or genuinely protecting the traditions they claim to champion, they are following the money and choosing to turn a blind eye.

To increase volume, there are corners one can cut. In Oaxaca there is a name for dodgy mezcals: *mezcales conejos. Conejo* means 'rabbit', because those mezcals are made so damn fast that they proliferate like rabbits. The spirit can be watered down way more than it should. Someone might say that there are a certain number of kilos (pounds) of *silvestres* in a mezcal when there are really only a few. Another surprisingly common one (that also strips the *tiñas* of their natural yeasts) is to add sodium bicarbonate to the fermentation to cut the time it takes by half. The hot new popular brands, often coming in below 40% ABV, will mix together batches of mezcal from many *palenques*, some that use all these techniques. And then print 'artisanal' on the bottle.

But what is most damaging about this is how it affects the local community. A *mezcalero* is taking these shorts to make more volume, which brings in more money. In the extra-tight-knit communities where mezcal is made, this does *not* go unnoticed. How is another *mezcalero* supposed to resist? Those extra bucks could go a long way. They have families, responsibilities.

This situation will corrode the culture faster than anything. And just so some hipster brand owners can feel good about themselves. When they promote their mezcals as helping the community, what they're really asking is that the community should help them make money.

A healthy environment

THE SOLUTION: SUSTAINING THE CULTURE AND THE LAND

The idea of scaling up something that is, by its nature, a craft product is inherently problematic. But there is always a best way forward and a number of cooperatives, producers and brands are working in earnest, intelligently trying to preserve mezcal's traditions while it rapidly expands today.

Some have begun and are finding other routes besides that of the dubious 'artisanal' stew (see page 33). One sound technique is to build a series of dedicated replica *palenques* next door to the 'mother' *palenque* that produces your successful signature spirit. This is then, ideally, overseen by the master *mezcalero*, creator of the original. It seems to work well, achieving a uniform flavour at a high volume.

Another way to scale up is to source other producers with whom, in terms of flavour and practices, you see eye-to-eye, thereby increasing your range and your volume while also representing the possibilities of the category and its terroir. Win-win.

But progress is not only about scaling up. Sustaining the environment while using traditional methods at the far higher output required is proving more and more difficult. Until recently, these were not such intense issues. But with the new extent of demand, they sure are now.

A PLATONIC IDEAL: SANZEKAN

Care for the ecology surrounding mezcal has been at the forefront in some regions for some time. As early as 1996, the incomparable Guerreran cooperative, Sanzekan, made reforestation, the health of their soil and the quality of the water a priority. For every tenth plant harvested, they let the eleventh flower and collected the seeds, mindful to plant again without disturbing the surrounding ecology, to retain soil structure. They collect water and they work with biologists to ensure a healthy balance to their work. It's central to the philosophy. And one that has been in place for as long as anyone can remember. In 1995, a team of Mexican environmentalists concerned about the health of natural resources in Guerrero decided to get a gauge by working with and studying mezcal producers in the state. What they expected to find was an ad hoc system at best. What they actually discovered was a highly organized and effective system of production and land management going back as far as the 1700s, and that it was still in place and being monitored and maintained by the entire community today.

Sanzekan, as a collective, has more than sixty *mezcaleros* working in forty-four *fabricas*, some of which are what's called *communitario*, meaning they're open for community use. Despite making mezcals in the exact manner that they have always done and only exporting between two hundred and four hundred litres (forty-four and ninety gallons) a year, Sanzekan the group and the adjoining brand are financially secure. This business model sits opposite to the philosophy of nearly every other brand. Sanzekan remains unregistered for export and wishes to remain that way, as they feel it not only threatens the community structure but the quality of the mezcals. What they have achieved suggests that mezcal, in its time-tested state, can sustain a whole community and, in fact, the pressures facing the culture come from individuals looking to profit through export. As Judah Kupah of family-owned brand Vago (see page 180) asserts, mezcal is already sustainable, we just have to leave it that way. We don't have to brand up, as CRM suggests. There are other ways of making an honest living, as is.

HOMECOMING

And those ways are, in fact, increasing. Certainly, one of the most positive developments for the community is the creation of gainful work for the young. Work with the added gravitas of something to be proud of. For the last generation or two, the perceived glamour of life in the USA was too persuasive to keep young men and women from heading North. The effect on families and communities and the individuals themselves has been productive in some regards, but disorienting, and, in tightly knit rural regions where mezcal is strongest, palpably corrosive.

But where, in the past, grandfather's work was seen as old-fashioned and irrelevant, it is beginning to turn the other way. With über-stylish bar folk from around the world coming to marvel at their ancestors' craft and heritage, and the ability to monitor through the internet the responses far, far away, dignity and self-respect has returned and has enveloped agave spirits.

HOW YOU CAN HELP

As an agave spirits enthusiast, your choices, wherever you live, can make a difference. A case in point is the story of NOM 186.

NOM 186 was a particularly cynical law that the bigger mezcal and tequila brands tried to push through government to force those mezcal producers *who were not part of the DO* to stop calling their mezcals 'mezcals'. But that's not all. The law also stipulated that they were not to, in any way, use the word 'agave' either. Crazy. In fact, the administration supervising the DOs claimed the word 'agave' as intellectual property… Behold, the depths to which people can stoop.

Anyhow, as you might expect, some people took issue with this. The majority of whom, significantly, lived abroad. Bar-people, journalists, everyday enthusiasts like you and I. They joined forces and petitioned and, to the unexpected relief of *mezcaleros* everywhere, had it overturned. What was learned from this is that when the market speaks — and 70% of agave spirits are exported — the Mexican industry listens.

The choices we make at the bar and the liquor store make a big difference. If blends of God-knows-what mixed at 38% ABV (see page 34) are flying off the shelves in the international sphere, then blends of God-knows-what mixed at 38% ABV is what we're going to get more of. Think about it.

The wet and wooded hills of Michoacán

INTERVIEW WITH REINA, A *MEZCALERA*

My grandfather and I worked on mezcal together for many years. My mom left me and went off to work with my dad when I was six months old. So my grandpa came to get me and I grew up with him. And we worked making mezcal. Right there. Behind that house over there.

My grandpa would go to the *palenque* and us little *chamaquitos* went to help him stoke the fire. We helped him with the pots. He had a *canoa* made from a wooden trunk the size of a mattress, and we would help him fill it. We would gather the *bagasso* and fill buckets with it, and when they were full, we would take them to him and he would toss them into the *tiñas* and we'd go back and fill 'em again.

When he went off to the fields to sow, he would leave us with firewood, and we would stay there stoking the fire. When the pot had been in the fire for a good three hours, it began to hiss, and we had to empty it, fill it up again and then add again more firewood. Like that. We filled one and emptied it, filled, emptied. We loved it. We had to deal with the jug full of mezcal, and we'd separate it out with a funnel better to be able to move it; we were that small.

It was a copper still. We don't mess around with clay pots here. They're dangerous! Many of my friends have told me I should use them, but I just don't have the patience for it. I'll barely get fifteen litres (three gallons) a day that way! And they're fragile and can break, too.

Back in the day, we had other types of agave around here. But we have lost a bunch of them now. We lost our *mexicano*. It was all *mexicanos* around here as far as the eye could see. My grandpa could get a ton of mezcal out of one of those plants. Up came the *maguey* and he would harvest it and take the mezcal from the plant. We had a lot of plants in our fields. We planted beans, maize, all kinds of crops. Still do.

Now I do most of the work. And I haven't gotten tired of working yet, either. This guy, a brickmaker, he comes to work with me. I do the stirring, and he mashes, and there you go.

I've got two kids, and they both left to live in the United States. Seeing as they're up there, well, I just take care of my fields. I want my good-looking little guys to be well off. The truth is, as they've been up there twelve years now, my kids don't know anything about making mezcal. I wouldn't recognize my son if he came back. Wouldn't even know who he was. When they'll come home, I don't know. He told me, "One day I'm going to come down." But still no. They don't know the treasure they have down here. I have the best mezcal.

I don't understand how my mezcal is so tasty. I go to the *palenques* of all our friends around here and we sit and we drink. But I prefer mine.

Maestra *Reina at home on her* palenque *in Miahuatlán, Oaxaca*

RITUAL

THE MEZCAL
EXPERIENCE

Mezcal is an experience. Whether we're knocking it back and blazing through the night, or relishing sips in lone contemplation, it's not passive. We are engaged. And there are a number of rituals we can undertake to heighten that experience.

The Zapotecs of the Oaxaca Valley, before taking a sip, raise their cups, pour some to the ground and say *dexeebe* (pronounced 'tidgibé'). This acknowledges the elements, the Sun and Earth, for giving life, and this moment, here and now, holding this treasured mezcal. The Zapotecs of the high sierra say *schesnichiu*, 'with permission from God and all those present'. It acknowledges that, in drinking mezcal, we are administering a sacrament.

I once found, in an old *National Geographic* magazine, an article about the Huichole that described how both Father Peyote (see page 20) and agave spirits were used by them in ceremonial practice. It meant a lot to me, this news. It confirmed something I had felt since my first sip: that mezcal worked on a number of different levels, including the spiritual.

I turned 37 in the New Year of 2007 when I took my first sip of mezcal. I was in Playa del Carmen to DJ. We'd been gigging about the planet for five years and I was exhausted. Five months before, my wife and I had separated. Our daughter was six. I was years away from being able to make sense of it, free-falling, but had found my way into Native American ceremony, the start of a new way forward. Alejandro Gamez, who went on to bottle Papadiablo and to be my first mezcal mentor, handed me a glass. Try this. At once, I knew it was good. It was a kind of relief. A part of me woke up and made an instant connection with the mezcal.

I should point out here that, though I sound an awful lot like one, I don't consider myself a New Agey kind of person. Which made the shock of such a realization – plant consciousness, in this case – all the more profound.

~

One night, years later, I found myself sitting by a small fire in a vast North-eastern Mexican desert, where those two sacraments, peyote and mezcal, were once again brought into ritual. A cup was raised and prayers were offered: to the elements, the four compass points, and then to The Fireplace himself. Boof! Up it went as the spirit was thrown on the fire, momentarily illuminating everything around us: the agave and the cactus, living together side by side. It had all come together at last.

Making mezcal in the community

Mezcal, orange slices, sal de gusano

THE JUDGE

If you're drinking in a group, it's nice to have one person doing the pouring. It definitely feels right and, conversely, all kinds of wrong if someone breaks out and just helps themselves. There has to be some order, a little formality, an etiquette: a ritual. Like the practice of the Japanese with sake. It's somehow in tune.

At Oaxacan weddings, where there can be, and often are, hundreds of people – the whole community present – mezcal is poured by what are called *jaices* or judges. One pours for all and we sip and go up together at the same time, experiencing similar sensations at a similar pace, hence enjoying each other's company all the more. Rather like we used to in nightclubs in younger days. Because of how many people there are, a number of judges are allotted, one for each table or group.

When someone requests another mezcal, they ask and it is poured by the *jaice*, who will need to pour one for themselves at the same time. It can lead to quite a lot of mezcal going down, especially for the judge, and so, I'm told, it's often women who are designated *jaices* as they handle their liquor better than men!

Mezcal is present at all the major milestones in the life of someone from a mezcal-making community: weddings, births, deaths, baptisms, birthdays, holidays... *todas las fiestas*. It's part of the fabric of community life. Or, as Jon Barbieri of Pierde Almas (see page 171) puts it, 'Mezcal is woven into the very tapestry of all of one's life.'

¡SALUD!

But, of course, mezcal, true to its paradoxical nature, is both sacred and secular, and so we can also simply — for the sake of the everyday — raise a glass, look our friends in the eye and say '¡Salud!' A toast to everyone's good health.

Orange slices are often served on the side, sprinkled with worm salt: a winning mix of dried *gusano*, chillies and salt. The salt has more tradition than the oranges, which were introduced in the mid-2000s as a way to define mezcal as other to tequila and her lemons. But it is also a welcome way to freshen up after a few. Delicious and just the complement to your bowl of *chapulines*: grasshoppers (I dread to think of the harvesting process) doused in chilli sauce and baked until crispy, tasting like delicately spiced, meaty, bite-sized Weetabix.

Tequila has unfairly been lumped with the practices of wayward Spring-Breakers, whose rite of passage relies on the 'slamming' of the lowliest fuel. But refined tequila is sipped and served with *sangrita* on the side. Made from tomato juice, lime juice and spices, *sangrita* is an elegant way of making your sipping cup long without mixing the spirit and masking its flavours.

~

There are cocktails, of course (see pages 184–218), and mezcals best suited to wrap up a dinner with wine. But ideally an evening out on solely the *puro-puro* is the thing to explore. Just be sure to eat plenty before you get going. The mezcal trail can get a little jazzy a little too quickly if one isn't careful. Much more so with mezcal than anything else, I've found.

It all lies in the stimulation-to-power ratio. With mezcals, we're able to drink a whopping amount of ABV because of the support we get from its stimulating nature. The risks this implies are considerable. The Attack of the Zombie *Mezcalero* is not pretty. Animated by the mezcal's unique stimulation, we can find ourselves feeling hardly as if we've drunk anything at all… but one minute you're more there than you've ever been; next minute, you are gone. The problem is, it's a whole other kind of gone. On any other drink we'd just capsize, but with the stimulation, you're completely out to lunch while still walking around physically functioning. It's one of the most disturbing things you can witness in your friends. Please, beware.

~

The greatest risk, as I say, comes from not eating enough. With the right amount of food in your tummy, you can slow the pace at which alcohol hits your brain. In Oaxaca, I start the night with a *tlayuda*, the local equivalent to our kebab, but with far better ingredients than the ones I used to munch post-pub, back home.

And then, suddenly, it's the morning after. Or sometimes midday. My friend Señor Ibarra always takes a *coctelle*. 'A Bloody Mary?', I asked. 'No, not that sort of *coctelle* but *mariscos*: shrimp, prawn, that sort of thing. Refreshing.' A good call. Me, being the Brit that I am, I go for soup. The Oaxacan soup is called *pozolé* and is just the thing.

NOTES ON TASTING

As we approach a mezcal for the first time, we might consider it as new terrain. A landscape with certain features we're looking to explore. What are they? What promises do they hold?

But first, let's pour a cup. Or a glass. Glass is less forgiving, more honest. *Jicaras* (gourd cups), though they look wonderful and bounce when you drop them, suck up some of the flavours, 'steal' them, as it was described to me. Clay *copitas* soften the mezcal, enhancing certain aspects, which can be pleasant. But, to get to the stark truth, use a glass.

And a wide-rimmed glass is best. Though it looks a bit odd, giant wine goblets are great. Mezcal has a fantastically broad vista and you want to allow for the full view. Wide-screen. IMAX mezcal. Though if there isn't one at hand, then a classic shot glass will do just fine. OK, so it's in the glass. Now swirl it about. Watch for the legs. Like in wine, neat rows and straight lines – long legs – indicate a good sugar structure, which suggests a healthy experience.

And how does it look? Clear or tinted? Subtle tints to the distillate can indicate certain things. Some good, some bad. A little yellowing might mean it's corked. A little green and it could mean super-legit as it's pure craft from a simple copper still. Most are crisp and crystal-clear unless they are *reposados* (see page 88), of course, and therefore amber.

Then, there is the texture. Dip your fingertips into the glass and rub a little on the back of your hand. Is it viscous? A sign of nice, flavour-conducting oils. Or perhaps it's not so oily. Fewer oils can mean a lighter, fresh-tasting mezcal and a good energetic lift. What you don't want is sugars that make your hand sticky. Those are not agave sugars. If they're in your mezcal, I suggest pouring it down the drain and finding another.

~

So then, to the nose. What aromas do you find? Surprisingly, it seems to me at least, almost all the flavours we discern are through the olfactory system. Try holding your nose and taking a sip: you'll get almost nothing. The tongue only recognizes five essential tastes: sweet, on the front of the tongue; salt, sour, umami and bitter on the sides and back.

It's with the nose that we're tasting, really. And I was told by a slightly genius German distiller, who makes gin for The Queen, that we are able to recognize all things in the material world this way. Thousands of flavours. Everything we've experienced. The trick is to make the connection between the flavour sensed and the memory. It's a leap made in the realm of synaesthesia and very satisfying when you pull it off, so give it a go.

Take a deep breath and clear your mind. Now, slowly move the cup from side to side about an inch beneath your nose. Notice how the aromas change, or at least become more defined in one specific place. There: that is the peak of your nasal power. Work from there, but go easy and only gently inhale – more a microscopic breathing in – or you might numb the nerves in your nostrils along with your ability to discern one mezcal from another for the rest of the evening. And get a red hooter while you're at it.

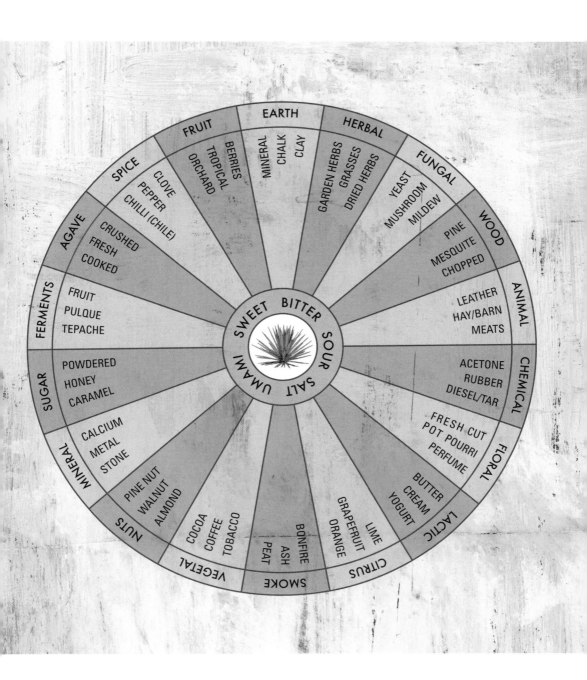

Now it's time to taste. Again, prepare yourself. You might want to reset your olfactory gear by resting your nose on your forearm for a moment. Inhale there and recognize the neutrality of your own skin. Now, return to the glass, breathe in and take a sip. A healthy amount. Let it pass across your tongue to the back of your mouth, then, as you swallow, slowly exhale through your nose. This adds oxygen to the mix and opens out all the flavours. *Bueno*. Now relax. What do you see?

~

It comes in colours, at first. A dab of purple, perhaps. With time you'll realize that was lavender. Or perhaps there's green. Slowly allow the mind to discern that it is, in fact, grasses. Furthermore, perhaps they're freshly chopped or just damp, or a suburban lawn thick with daisies. Relax, have fun and blurt out whatever comes to you. It's all a process of matching up the tastes, the aromas and your past experiences. It's not easy, but you do get the hang of it and — when someone calls out what they're getting and you get it, too — it's super-satisfying.

I once sat in a tasting group in New York. There were two full-on wine critics among us. We sipped and one calmly called the presence of leather. The other responded with, 'Yes, black,' and then, after a short pause, 'Wet'. Mhmmm, yes. Murmurs of accord from the group. Then the former summarized the meeting of their minds with: 'Black, wet, saddle leather... New.' And there it was, clear as day, the object, in the mind's eye. Try it at home. It's such fun.

~

Having said all that, I must admit that of ultimate importance to me is the way the mezcals make us feel. I see the fact that they are sublimely delicious and endlessly varied and come from an inspiringly deep and rich culture as some blessed by-product. Like medicine, I happily would drink them if they tasted awful.

~

Just as with all the different flavours, there are any number of ways mezcals can affect you. I was once running a tasting in London for a group of bloggers and bar-folk when one bright Irish lady piped up and exclaimed, as if in astonishment, 'They're all different frequencies!' Eureka. She had nailed it. Frequencies. Like musical notes that create different energies inside of us. The basis of sound healing. It's the same phenomena at the root of tasting mezcal. So, next time you're at a *mezcaleria*, once you really start to get your chops down and learn the bottles and the regions, the productions and the plants, you can play one off against the other. Play your energies like musical notes. Up, down. How do I feel? Where do I want to go next?

I asked the lady: 'What note is this?' She replied, 'E flat?' (This is a true story.) I said, 'Sure. Was that one G?' 'Yeah,' she said, 'And that one…' pointing to the Papadiablo Especial, a mezcal made from four different plants (see page 166), '…was a chord.'

MEZCALERIAS

The *mezcaleria* in Mexico is more than just a bar. It is part community centre; part place of study. Part sanctuary; part gang hut. Part church; part place for celebrations.

Wonderfully, today there are more and more great *mezcalerias* springing up around the globe. Places with broad selections and informed bar staff who have visited the *palenques* and know what they're talking about.

Here's some recommendations, places worldwide that are championing mezcal. Drop into one near you.

Mezcaloteca, Oaxaca

AKADEMI

Katamama Hotel, Jl Petitenget No 51B,
Seminyak, Bali 80361, Indonesia
www.akademi-bar.com

As the name suggests, Akademi is a place of
learning. An unusual place where the public are
invited to roll up their shirt sleeves and follow
the academic path. As a *mezcaleria*, it's also
unusual in that it doesn't have any mezcal.

But bar manager Dre Masso's thinking
is all mezcalogical. He spent 2004 under the
tutelage of Julio Bermejo in San Francisco and
explored Mexico that same year, then returned
to London to open the infamous Green and Red
Cantina which, at the time, had the largest
selection of tequilas and mezcals in Europe.
The successful venture ran for a full five years
and, during that time and upon subsequent
forays across the border, Dre absorbed the
mezcalero outlook on region and terroir. This he
now applies to the world of Indonesian arak.

So if it's not a *mezcaleria*, why the
mention? Well, it does carry a number of
bottles. And, if you're in Indonesia, it may
be your only hope. But the main reason to
mention Akademi is in the spirit of applying
what we learn from mezcal culture to other
spirits. Immersing ourselves in small-batch,
community-based, regional spirit production
brings us closer to the natural rhythms of life.
Dre gets this, and is spreading the outlook to
positive effect in other parts of the world (next
stop, his ancestral roots in Colombia).

Rather than altering mezcal, the thing
that inspires us, we can learn to work with
what we love in the way it wants us to, in
healthy exchange.

ARCHIVO MAGUEY

Murguia 218, Esquina Reforma, Oaxaca, Mexico
www.archivomaguey.com

I have, once or twice, I admit, considered in
a lazy, abstract kind of way what it might be
like inside the molecular realm of an agave.
An evening in Archivo Maguey is, I expect, a
close glimpse.

En primero, it's the use of the space.
The wide open rooms on the second floor,
with views of the *Calle* Reforma rushing past,
are sparsely adorned with cosmic detail, the
art work of Chucho, manager and part-owner,
along with his mum and dad. Chucho also built
the altar-like pyramidal bars, back-bars and
stools; the combined effect is other-worldly and
all one hundred per cent agave inspired.

Chucho and his family are from the
North-western tip of Oaxaca, Mixteco country,
a tight-knit, seldom-visited region with a
wealth of mesmerizing mezcals. All the mezcals
at Archivo are sourced from the region and
made from endemic, unusual and delicious
agaves. For example, a tiny *tobalá* that is so
sweet that it yields more mezcal than its larger
cousin and tastes of lavender. A delicate, sweet
lavender mezcal, in this case. But to Chucho
and his family — and to *mezcaleros* of the
Mixtec — flavours are secondary, just part of the
expression of the agave plants' power. Mezcals
are medicines, healing and guiding.

As a way to connect with the cosmic
realities of mezcal culture, I can't recommend
a better place to go (order the phenomenally
good *tlayuda insectos* while you're there), and
perhaps catch for yourself a glimpse within the
molecular realm of an agave.

'Menu for the week', Archivo Maguey, Oaxaca

BAD SPORTS

184 Hackney Rd, London E2 7QL, UK
www.badsports.co.uk

The city of Puebla was built by the Spanish on the site of Cholula which, at the time – 1532 – was the largest man-made pyramid in the world. In Mexico, there are a number of examples of one civilization building their temple directly on top of another. Bad Sports continues that tradition on Hackney Road, having rebuilt the agave altar on the hallowed ground where *mezcaleria* QuiQuiRiQui once stood. (Mysteriously, both I and Jon Anders of Amathus Drinks, the mezcal importer, once lived within feet of here.)

Blow your mind with incredible *puro-puro*, while relishing the fact that you're in one of the best-named *mezcalerias* of all time.

BAR CLANDESTINO

13 Boulevard du Temple, 75003 Paris, France
www.1k-paris.com/fr

There are plenty of spots in Paris that carry mezcal, but this bar is 100% agave.

It's headed up by part-owner, part-Mexican and original spark David Migueres, who felt compelled to return to Oaxaca to live with producers, learning the ropes and studying the craft of mezcal-making himself. He knows more than most in Paris about the culture.

The setting is smart: Oaxaqueño meets Parisian, and it is magical to sip from the rustic Mexican soil in such surroundings… especially when the bar is hidden secretly in the back of the 1K Hotel in the Marais.

THE BARKING DOG

Sankt Hans Gade 19, 2200 Nørrebro,
Copenhagen, Denmark
www.thebarkingdog.dk

I was tipped off about this bar on a DJing trip to Copenhagen. I made the pilgrimage and was blown away. The quality of the mezcals was, at the time – 2010 – hard to match or even to acquire outside Mexico. The barman casually knew his stuff. I wished I lived in Copenhagen. This was far more fun and closer to the way things went in Mexico then anything I could find in New York.

Some years later, I got chatting with a chap at a bar show in Berlin. He was wearing a RUN:DMC tee-shirt that was switched out to say MEZ:CAL. Genius, really.

I produced, from under my jacket, a bottle of Papadiablo. We shared a sip and our stories. It transpired this was Carl Wrangel, Danish mezcal pioneer and proprietor of the Copenhagen bar I'd fallen for a few years back. Needless to say, I bought a tee.

BRAHMS & LISZT

10 Chatsworth Road, London E5 0LP, UK
www.brahmsandlisztlondon.uk

Brahms & Liszt, as you may know, in rhyming slang, means 'pissed' (as in drunk). The magnificent Melanie Symmonds does it again. She remains one of my favourite proponents of all-things-agave this side of the Mexican border. MS re-opens doors and bottles to the public under another brilliant moniker and the single roof of her offie / mezcal school.

This is, in a way, the reincarnation of the legendary *mezcaleria* QuiQuiRiQui which still stands, in my book, as the closest any bar I have visited has got to the wild and easy feeling of a fine Mexican *mezcaleria*.

Now, high-brow meets good times once more in the hands with the golden touch. She knows her stuff and how to share mezcal with appropriate abandon.

An earnest aficionado, Melanie earned her chops with not only the bar, but also by bottling the first British mezcal brand of the same name, QuiQuiRiQui (see page 172). This place is worth a visit. Come for the mezcal; stay for the tasting.

BRILLIANT CORNERS

470 Kingsland Rd, London E8 4AE, UK
www.brilliantcornerslondon.co.uk

What do John Coltrane, Walter Gibbons and *madrecuixe* all have in common? Brilliant Corners. Amit and Anish Patel, two rather brilliant brothers, have housed jazz, disco and mezcal in dark woods, easy vibes and a Klipschorn sound-system on the Kingsland Road. It makes for a great evening out. Starting with dining on fine Japanese fare and ending with all-out hands-in-the-air blazing it out on the dance floor. All fuelled by top *puro-puro* mezcals. Brilliant indeed.

Clockwise from main picture: Espita, Washington, DC; Bar Clandestino, Paris; Del 74 Taqueria, London; Tentacion, Berlin

CAFÉ PACIFICO

5 Langley St, London WC2H 9JA, UK
www.cafe-pacifico.com

The dictionary defines an institution as 'a society or organization founded for a religious, educational, social, or similar purpose'.

We could say it was, to some extent, all three and/or certainly similar in purpose. For one, owner – and official tequila ambassador to Europe – Tom Estes works with a near-religious stamina and constancy to further the world of agave spirits, gathering many disciples, myself included, along the way. His ability to proselytize comes naturally, as Estes started his career as a teacher. There's not a person outside Mexico who can speak as eloquently about agave spirits as he.

Socially, the place has been a hub for all sorts of folk for four decades. From modest beginnings in Amsterdam in 1976 – established as a way of participating in the overwhelming free-thinking social wave of the era – it went on to take hold in eighteen other cities around the world. That has to be a lot of socializing and a million or more margaritas.

But the Café Pacifico in Covent Garden, London, is, of all of them, the mothership. Set up in 1982 at a time when the only Mexican restaurants in the city were of the 'white-tablecloth' variety, it is likely the earliest bar to serve mezcal in the country. (While in 1978, an importation undertaken by Tom was probably the first into Europe.)

As an institution, it's hard to get closer to the dictionary definition. And for a great mezcal in central London, it's hard to do better.

CASA MEZCAL

86 Orchard Street, New York NY 10002, USA
www.casamezcalny.com

Occasionally, I Heart New York. I lived there for 20 years. And was in a punk band that used to play the Lower East Side, my neighbourhood. We played a song called 'New New York'. Back then you couldn't get a mezcal if you knew what it was to want one in the first place. Casa Mezcal is now serving *mezcales* in the old neighbourhood and is my favourite place to get mezcal, now that I know what it is.

These days there's a lot of mezcal in the Big Apple. And all kinds of different ways to enjoy it. For the longest time, it was served in mostly the fancy variety of restaurants that present extraordinarily beautiful dishes and drinks that are far removed from the rural, rough-around-the-edges places in which mezcals are made.

Which is why, when in NYC, I head to the old neighbourhood for a bar that reminds me of Oaxaca, my new neighbourhood.

THE CHUG CLUB

Taubenstraße 13, 20359 Hamburg, Germany
+49 40 35735130

I once had a friend who used to cry 'chug-chug-chug' when he became overexcited on an evening of mezcal. He got the nickname Spring Break because of it.

Not an enlightening anecdote at first glance, only he was the owner of a mezcal company that only bottled especially distinguished clay-pot mezcals.

I always loved seeing these two contradictory forms of mezcal-in-action, working this deeply knowledgeable human being into a frenzy: the exquisitely sophisticated and eternally primal.

The Chug Club in Hamburg similarly encourages its clientele to 'chug', only perhaps not so literally. Owner Betty Kupsa – who must know a good name when she sees one – invented the Chug Club as a way of connecting reluctant drinkers with what she knew they would love: agave spirits.

By halving the pourage, dropping the price, coining the great handle and providing herself with a hundred-plus *mezcales*, it was impossible to fail.

They are open seven days a week and have dedicated Mondays solely to the imbibing of what they call 'the most sexy spirit': mezcal. Who could resist?

CUISH

Diaz Ordaz 712, Center, Oaxaca, Mexico
www.mezcalescuish.com

Oaxaca City *centro* is really two centres, each gathered around a different church. The one in the North, Santa Domingo, is nestled in the more bougie end of things. The Cathedral in the *zocalo* and the streets South of that are much more for your everyday working Oaxaqueño. Not so big on the fancy crafts. More tyre (tire) shops, cheap jeans and a block full of hookers. One block on from that and you're at Cuish.

Cuish is an oasis. Not just in the rowdy nabe but in the field of *mezcalerias*, too. It's super-dignified, gorgeously designed, open and mellow, with two floors, two bars and plenty

of space to do your thing, but most attractive to me is that it's full of locals. And, of course, equally full of great mezcals.

Felix, the owner, grew up in Oaxaca and into the mezcal life. He's young and inspired and that is reflected in his bar and his capacity to question and reframe the common understandings of mezcal culture.

The place has plenty of stunning artwork by the city's radical contemporary print-work movement. And great music gently pumped from a home-made speaker system hanging from the ceiling. Local beers and great *tlayudas*. Make the trip. Cross the tracks.

DEL 74

87 Lower Clapton Road, London E5 0NP, UK
www.facebook.com/Tacosdel74

'OK, so just so you know, I'm opening the first Taqueria Bar Del 74 at the end of this month, and looks like I'll be opening another one at the beginning of March, and possibly another one in the summer. So things are pretty freaking hectic at the moment.' I loved receiving this email. Firstly, good news. Secondly, it cracks me up when Enrique gets serious. He and I are mates. He's from Veracruz, hence the grammar. We both lived in New York in the 1990s and went to the same parties. That creates a bond. As does the mezcal. Which is how we met formally. He owns Boho Mexica on Commercial Street in London. His auntie makes the food. I went by for a tasting. And stayed for hours. His new operation, Taqueria Bar Del 74, promises to be all stripped down: *tacos, chelas y mezcal*. Looking forward to it.

DR ROTTERDAM

Secret location, Rotterdam, The Netherlands
+31 6 3131 4446
www.drrotterdam.com

Mezcal is medicine. And when in Holland, Arno van Eijmeren, aka Dr Rotterdam, is your man. There's a number of ways to get to see the doctor. For the private bar, simply known as Dr, you'll need an appointment. For the dispensary, an outlet for your cocktail needs, walk-ins are welcome. Either way, there's plenty of agave love to keep us all ticking over nicely.

EL DESTILADO

5 de Mayo 409, Oaxaca 68000, Mexico
www.eldestilado.com

It's hard to imagine this *mezcaleria*, which provides one of the warmest welcomes in Oaxaca, having spent its nascent year under wraps, a speakeasy hidden under everyone's noses. Now, the doors are wide open and the bar sits practically on the street a block from Santa Domingo in *el centro*, Oaxaca.

But it was under such circumstances that young American Jason Cox began circulating the extraordinary mezcals he amassed on excursions about the country in search of the unusual.

Five Sentidos are the fruits of that search (see page 138) and though, outside this bar, they are not easy to find, they're worth hunting down. Behind the bar is a range of twenty or so. But you need to move fast as they come and go quickly: batches average only in the region of fifty litres (eleven gallons).

EL PASTÓR

6–7A Stoney St, London SE1 9AA, UK
www.tacoselpastor.co.uk

In the late 1990s, Sam Hart and Crispin Somerville opened a nightclub in downtown Mexico City. They did this, Crispin explains, so that, basically, no one could throw them off the decks. The club, El Colmillo, took off, and became a stronghold for electronic music.

During the Colmillo years, a steady stream of folk would show up with samples of radical mezcals and *raicillas*. It was not something Hart or Somerville forgot and now, 20 years later, it is being succinctly expressed in El Pastór, their tidy new home in London's Borough Market.

They have a discerning selection of imports and a house mezcal selected from Palenque Milagrito.

ESPITA

1250 9th St NW, Washington, DC 20001, USA
www.espitadc.com

Espita takes mezcal seriously. They understand the nuances of the spirit and its origins in a way that, quite possibly, only those from outside a culture are able to. I'm thinking of the way that hip-hop is to the Japanese and jazz to the Europeans. This can make for a meticulous attention to detail, which Espita does flawlessly. It also may prove essential to mezcal's preservation as it goes global.

Staff at Espita are required not only to visit Oaxaca but to work on every stage of mezcal production. The policy on what they stock is based on the most rigorous set of standards for sustainability that I've come across. Also, nothing below 43% ABV. (That they have 130 mezcals in stock says a lot about the quality of the American import market.) For such a large-scale (74 seats for dining) and high-profile establishment (10 blocks from the White House) to hold such standards, I like to think, will make for positive effects at home and abroad. Whichever way round that is for you. Go show some support.

GALLO PÉLON

106 S Wilmington St, Raleigh, NC, 27601, USA
www.gallopelon.com

I've never met Marshall Davis, bar manager at Gallo Pélon, but I'd like to. He wrote:

'Gallo Pélon is the first (and only as of now) *mezcaleria* in the Carolinas. We opened in March 2015 and carry over 60 *mezcales*. North Carolina is a highly controlled state, so acquiring this volume of mezcal was/is a huge undertaking. I try to only carry quality, artisanal *mezcales*. We do keep one industrial mezcal on the shelf for those who want to try it in comparison. We highly support responsible, sustainable producers, and our goal is to visit the *palenque* of one of our brands per year.'

Many of the *mezcalerias* listed in these pages have a similar outlook. Their work with the spirit inspires them to take care of it. It's in the nature of mezcal. It asks you, somehow, to ask, and this leads to a way of running a bar that works wonderfully for all. I liked the way Mr Davis put it, so I thought I'd print this.

Gallo Pélon, North Carolina

In Sítu, Oaxaca

IN SÍTU

Av Morelos 511, Oaxaca, Mexico
www.insitumezcaleria.com

Mezcal is for drinking. But at the same time, there's so much to learn, it's addictive. I often head out to the *mezcaleria* simply to try and find out more. Oddly, as my Spanish is so bad and English is not an option, I've learnt more at In Sítu than at all the other *mezcalerias* I frequent. Sitting there, at the bar, with Ulises and Sandra, one seems able to grasp in some intangible way the deepest meanings of the nature of mezcal. Which just might be, after all, beyond language.

 Sounds grandiose or far-fetched? But with their mixture of untamed knowledge, disarming nonchalant demeanour, a killer

soundtrack and my favourite range of mezcals under any one roof, something out of the ordinary is bound to happen.

LA CLANDESTINA

Alvaro Obregon 298, Mexico City, Mexico
www.milagrito.com

La Clandestina was one of the very first *mezcalerias* to open up in Mexico City and the first that I ever went to. In a way I consider it my local and when I go back it feels like a return home. There's a warmth to the place. The feeling is communal. The music is fun. The vibe is energetic. It feels like it's being steered by the whole room. A group endeavour, nice and unpredictable. You never know what's going to happen.

The whole back wall of the bar is made of giant glass flagons full of rad mezcals from across the country. But the best come from the environmentally sustainable *palenque* the owners built in Oaxaca, which is a shining example of how to produce a healthy volume of traditional mezcals at no cost to the land. The 30-odd mezcals are outlined in an ever-changing pamphlet.

LA MEZCALERIA

Carrer la Santa Creu, 3, 07800 Dalt Vila, Ibiza, Illes Balears, Spain
www.lamezcaleria.com

In 1990, I — madly as I was only 20 — became manager of a peculiar bar in Cambridge called The Blue Boar. Academics during the mornings, deadbeat friends in the afternoons… and chaos every night. Working here required the highest levels of integrity. Here I became friends with Adrian Fillary.

Now that he lives part of the year on the beautiful Northern coast of Ibiza — and is a regular at La Mezcaleria — I asked him to be my man on the ground.

'Small charming bar in the winding side streets in the castellated walled old town. Ceviche, sushi, guac and tacos to accompany cocktails, carafes and whole bottles of mezcal. A couple of pavement (sidewalk) tables outside. Friendly helpful staff. Small good selection of mezcals though I pretty much stick to Siete Misterios *arroqueño* and *tobalá*. Serve is with the orange slices and gubbins.'

And I believe him.

MAMASITA

Level 1/11 Collins St, Melbourne, Victoria 3000, Australia
www.mamasita.com.au

Any *mezcaleria* perched above a 7:11 'up a dodgy little staircase' would pique my interest. Though especially Mamasita. The owners lived and worked in Mexico and NYC before deciding to 'bring home the bits we loved most from our adventures'. Hence real mezcals and a 7:11. Good combo.

They also serve legit Mexican cuisine and, I understand, were the first to do so in mighty Oz. The staff are deeply knowledgeable on the subject of the spirits they serve, and seven nights of the week, one person is on hand solely to impart the good word on agave loving. A lot on offer.

MESA VERDE

Level 6, Curtin House, 252 Swanston Street, Melbourne, Victoria 3000, Australia
www.mesaverde.net.au

A place I have been to many times. There's a super-loose nightclub in the top floor of the same building, on the main drag in downtown Melbourne. The building is dedicated to fun stuff and the PAM Clothing family have kept stores there for years.

But, despite knowing it well, as my friend DJ Andee 'House de Frost' practically lives here, I thought I'd let him sum it up: 'Spaghetti westerns, southern hospitality and general stoogieness. It's worth the climb!!' *Soy en acuerdo*. Check it out.

Mezcaloteca, Oaxaca

MEZCALITO

2323 Polk Street, San Francisco, CA 94109, USA
www.mezcalitosf.com

Guadalupe Jaques is a man after my own heart. He knows mezcal – loves it – and runs a record label on the side. Furthermore, he can mix mezcal drinks that work wonders. I met him in his new position as bar manager here, in old Russian Hill out the back of Chinatown, San Francisco, a city for which I also have a soft spot, having lived there for five years in the early 1990s when that whole lounge-lizard, easy-listening boom came in. We'd dress in suits, don a little make-up and overdo it in vintage cars. It was a moment, a fun one, but since, I've never been interested in cocktails. Guadalupe and SF that afternoon brought it all back. Whether you're new to or experienced in mezcal or the city, check out Mezcalito and our man, Guadalupe.

MEZCALOTECA

Secret location, Oaxaca, Mexico
www.mezcaloteca.com

Mezcal, in its paradoxical way, is both celebratory and learned, an especially winning combination, I find. One of the great natural highs of the drink and culture is the stimulation offered by new information about it that, under the influence of agave spirits, can be a revelatory experience.

Mezcaloteca is not only one of the best places to undertake this kind of schooling, it was also the first to offer it.

The name is drawn from the Spanish for library, *biblioteca*, and you do indeed arrive into the hushed stillness of a place of study, lovingly detailed in dark woods, low-lit with brass lamps, and with hundreds of neatly labelled bottles in rows, like so many books on so many shelves, naturally inviting inquiry.

Though at first glance it may seem slightly gimmicky, there's nothing novel about it at all. The impulse to open Mezcaloteca came from a wish to teach.

Silvia Philion and Marco Ochoa found that their relationship with mezcal had developed into a passionate commitment. But, even in Oaxaca, the all-important and – at that time – unwritten knowledge of the *palenque* and its *maestros* was yet to find a bridge into town.

Today, the practice of listing on the label, in detail, the name of the producer, the region and the processes undertaken to make a mezcal is commonplace, even taken for granted. Mezcaloteca was the first to do it. To Silvia and Marco it was only logical. Their interest was just in getting the information across.

So now they had found their purpose, had the name worked out and the concept; next they found the location.

Mezcaloteca is a speakeasy, so to speak. You can't just rock up. It is by appointment only: a buzz at the door, an awkward moment as you're cleared on CCTV... and then you're in. It can add a sense of import to one's research, as if the world of traditional mezcals – as to some extent it probably does – depends on it.

Mezcolateca, Oaxaca

The tendency to want to teach, or pass on the knowledge we have, about mezcal culture, becomes, for many, incredibly strong. For Silvia and Marco, this is the primary focus of the bar. During your visit, you sit with a *maestro* of your own just as in school. You're encouraged to pursue any agave-based interests you have, or to sit back and relax and let your teacher walk you through it, delighting in amazing *mezcales* as you go.

If it all sounds a bit stiff, don't be put off. It's a rare pleasure and the incredible mezcals, representing near-every-possible permutation available within the culture, are, every one, phenomenal. In the calm of the library we are left to experience our silent ecstasies all the more profoundly.

MISCELÁNEA MEZCALERA

Avenida Mistral 15, 08015 Barcelona, Spain
www.miscelanea.info

Una miscelánea, in Mexico, is a little shop where you can get all the bits and bobs you need. Everyday stuff that you rarely think of but can't live without. Miscelánea Mezcalera supplies all those things for the *mezcaleros y mezcaleras* of Barcelona.

It's headed up by Carlos and Pedro, Oaxaqueños who decided that Barcelona, one of the best cities in which to enjoy good times, would benefit from fine *mezcales*. In 2012, they began to import, creating this place to connect with the drinks and their mother culture.

OJO ROJO

106 Commercial Road, The Triangle,
Bournemouth, BH2 5LR, UK
www.ojo-rojo.co.uk

Beyond the grand beachfront promenades of
Bournemouth is a funky part of town with a
tasty little record shop and a *mezcaleria* that
totally gets what the spirit of agave is about.

At the helm is Gemma Terry who has
fathomed mezcal culture. She describes her
first sip as a moment when she could picture
mezcal country: 'Colourful, bold, a little rough
around the edges, just like mezcal.' She's keen
to keep mezcal sustainable and chooses brands
involved in reforestation and biodiversity.

It's an inspired outlook and an inspiring
mezcaleria. A place Gemma describes as 'an
escape and an experience'. I'm there.

OPPA-LA

4F Enoshima View Tower, 1-12-17
Katasekaigan, Fujisawa, Kanagawa, Japan
251-0035

Oppa-la, a wooden gang-hut perched on the
lip above the Pacific Ocean on the coast of
Japan, is what mezcal is all about. Community,
creation, culture. Not to mention style, flavour
and good times.

It's equal part bar/dance floor/printing
press/food spot/community centre and, if
I could go anywhere tonight, it'd be there.

The owner, Daa, understands. If your
intentions are for the greater good of all, you
can't go wrong. It's mezcalife in action.

PS: did I mention the surf-break?

PALENQUE

13 E Louisiana, Denver, CO 80210, USA
www.palenquemezcaleria.com

The first time I tried to write about mezcal was
for a 'zine I made. I opened with the immortal
line: 'Mezcal changed my life'. My girlfriend
laughed and part of me felt foolish... but
another part knew it was true.

Palenque is a *mezcaleria* in Denver,
Colorado. It has a small-but-elegant Oaxaca-
inspired food menu along with a bumper range
of top *mezcales*. The owner emailed me and
said this:

'Agave spirits literally changed my
life. When I started to visit Mexico to see
the production and culture of mezcal,
I instantly wanted to be a better person.
Mezcal brings out the best in me. The culture
teaches hard work, passion, sustainability,
and an overall willingness to help others.
I take that philosophy and incorporate it
into my restaurants. I do not hire based
on experience. I hire my staff based on
the type of people they are. I hire based
on passion.

'Without having experienced
mezcal as much as I have, I do not believe
I would have successful businesses. Not
only do I translate what mezcal means to
me in the work place, but also at home.
I named my beautiful daughter after an
Agave Valenciana!'

I got goosebumps. Not only am I not
alone and – at last – validated; I felt when
I read it that, for the first time, one might be
able to believe that mezcal will survive in the
big wide world after all.

Oppa-La, Enoshima, Japan

Clockwise from main picture:
La Mezcaleria, Ibiza; Brahms and Liszt,
London; Mezcaloteca, Oaxaca;
bottles at Brahms and Liszt, London;
Bad Sports, London

Pare de Sufrir, Guadalajara

PARE DE SUFRIR

Calle Argentina 66, Americana, 44160
Guadalajara, Mexico
+52 33 3826 1041

Pare de Sufrir. 'stop suffering'. I certainly did.
In fact, I stopped suffering for just as long
as you possibly could, arriving before they'd
opened and being the last to leave. I'd heard
about the place for years and had finally, only
just, made it.

'Only just', because friends and I had
found ourselves in a car, four days prior,
heading East with a party of indigenous
Indians. The mission was successful; after
being initiated into the ancient ways, we'd
witnessed extraordinary beauty and truth
involving, among other things, mezcal.

Back, glowing and rested, I would not
have left the house for any old mezcaleria. But

Pare de Sufrir is an undisputed mecca. And the
pilgrimage was to be as eventful as the one
before… and possibly as psychedelic.

Straight off, it was the vibe. Local,
friendly, mixed (I wasn't the only silverback),
a solid community centre. Which it was in
appearance. A concrete, low-ceilinged,
square room. How I'd picture the gang hut
of a 1960s South American rebel organization.
Very cool, tons of simpatico, low-lit, smoky,
great music.

A band and a DJ. Everything was good.
Probably, in primero, as the mezcals are so very
damn good. Odd and stinky, organized by region
in a way that solicits inquiry. Our barman was a
star: patient.

I asked him about a bottle, a single
squat-looking number, that sat dead-centre,
high on the top shelf. 'This one is special,' he
tells me. 'Would you like to try?' and poured me

a tiny sip. 'We don't sell much 'cos it's twice the price of everything else.'

I sipped. Hmm... nice flavours nothing very un... whoa!... wait a minute. It was as if I had diamond zen clarity of the mind. The wipers had cleared the windshield. It felt like my two eyes had formed one great dish of vision: a third eye. It was a minor revelation.

Afterwards, I switched back to a *raicilla*. But what had been transportative before now felt murky, tiring and brought me down to earth. That mezcal had been the one. I took another. The DJ struck up and I danced like a bandit until close.

PS It was a *tepeztate* from Rey de Zapoteca of Santiago Matatlán. Lot 001.

QUIOTE

2456 N California Ave, Chicago, IL 60647, USA
www.quiotechicago.com

'There is a harmony that exists in a good glass of mezcal that escapes description.' Dan Salls and Paul Biasco, proprietors, understand what they're involved in, and that the best way to talk about it is to pour it.

Though first, of course, you have to know what's being said. And they learned through years of immersion exploring the 'interconnectedness' of *mezcalero* and agave, culture and land, before returning to build their multi-faceted 'ode to the agave' in Chicago's Logan Square nabe back home.

Good news, if you live in Chicago, and, for the price of an Uber, you can eat the food and drink the drink and connect with the Mexican earth seven days a week.

RHONDA'S

3–5 Kurrawyba Avenue, Terrigal, NSW 260, Australia
www.rhondas.bar

A measure of how universal the spirit of agave can be appeared in an email sent to me from a picturesque stretch of Eastern Australia coast, an idyll of sun and surf and the 30-year-running Rhonda's. The manager offered this:

'Our philosophy on agave spirits is to preserve the culture and heritage of the land it comes from, the people who make it and the traditions they live by, by supporting producers with ethics and integrity.'

SACAPALABRAS

Calle de Manuel García Vigil & Quetzalcoatl, número 104, Oaxaca de Juárez 68000, Mexico
+52 951 351 8371

There's no shortage of great places to drink mezcal in Oaxaca. I go to Sacapalabras for mezcal and jazz. Every night there's a blazing team of young Oaxaqueños giving it all they've got in raw, mezcal-fuelled sets. And the mezcal is no ordinary mezcal, but the clay-pot distillations from fourth-generation *mezcalero* 'Lalo', son of the *maestro* of Santa Catarina Minas, Lorenzo Angeles. It carries the *mezcaleria*'s name, Sacapalabras, sacred words, and there are many more behind the bar than are available to buy. Which are hard enough to find in the first place. With the jazz and the 'sensory' artwork, serious cuisine by the owner and Lalo's *mezcales*, it's a proper Oaxaca City-Now night out.

SUPER LOCO

60 Robertson Quay, 1–13 The Quayside,
Singapore 238252
www.super-loco.com

I love seeing mezcal at work in other parts of
the world. Completely out of context... but
unaffected. Consistently giving people that
agave glow that only mezcal and its sister
spirits can. Super Loco is a 'group' that has
three restaurants. The mezcals are popular.
And appreciated in a way that works for the
Singaporean crowd. Good old mezcal: patient
and understanding, generous and giving.

TENTACION

Scharnweber str 32, Berlin 10245, Germany
+49 30 23930401

Opened in 2015 by folk with Mexican roots.
A way to bring their family into their Berlin lives
and loves. Here's how they put it:

'We offer exclusively mezcal. It is part of
our lives. It has been with us in good times and
bad times. When you drink mezcal, you taste
tradition, sun, soil, love, time, culture, you taste
the very best life has to offer.'

Along with beer brewed-in-house, they
serve *pulque* (see page 22), as well. Tempted?

Super Loco, Singapore

TIO'S CERVECERIA

4–14 Foster St, Surry Hills NSW 2010, Australia
www.instagram.com/tioscerveceria

2011 — in terms of agave love international — is an age ago. Early doors. But Sydney was there and agave was being promoted by the crew at Tio's Cerveceria, along with good beer, of course. Emphasis on good times here. Beer helps, but agave love is all you need.

VOODOO CAFÉ

84 Skinnergate, Darlington, DL3 7LX, UK
www.voodoocafe.co.uk

In 2012, I did my first drinks trade show. My first time to do one, first time to attend one and — popping out the other side of a way-over-the-top two-day rave/wedding — I was so the worse for wear, the last time I ever wanted to. Though there was a highlight and that was meeting Les and Kendra from the Voodoo Café.

Mezcal is all heart and no pretence, unlike the drinks show, and they are cut from cloth that understands the ways of the agave intuitively. Few others were buying it by the case at the time. They loaded up and drove North to spread the good word.

Two years before that, Les and Kendra had once again acted intuitively and decided that Darlington, Teeside, needed a Latin bar. It proved a good move.

Their place has received a number of national and international awards for what it does and it offers some seriously good mezcals, along with, somewhat incongruously, salsa and tango dancing and live music events.

ZANDUNGA

Garcia Vigil 512E, Oaxaca de Juárez 68000, Mexico
+52 951 516 2265

Besides Alvaro's — where I go to eat *pozolé* three times a week and watch TV with all the Mexican families — Zandunga is my favourite place to have supper in Oaxaca. I'm no foodie, but I think I get what it's all about when I'm there. It's a rapturous experience. I'm taken away. The mezcals play their part.

Many of the Oaxaqueño *mezcalerias* work much like a brand. They source their own producers, buy in batches, bottle up and present from behind the bar. Any branded mezcals that make it to the shelf consider it a serious accolade, no matter how tucked out of the way they may be.

Zandunga, however, despite having its own sublime range of ten or so up on the chalk board, carries dozens and dozens of branded mezcals as well. It suggests support and encouragement to the brand owners who work hard to try and bring legit mezcals out into the marketplace. It would be in tune with the gracious nature of everyone who works there. The staff are all inherently aware of the qualities of each mezcal. Actually, much of my early schooling was undertaken there at the long bar, carved with the shapes of agaves.

TENTACIÓN
CRAFT BEER

MEZCALERÍA

CERVECERIA

SANKT HANS
THE DOG
PARKING

SACAPALABRAS
EXPENDIO GALERIA BAR

Calle de
Quetzalcóatl →

MEZ
CAL
+ SCANDINAVIAN AGAVE PROJECT +

*Clockwise from main picture:
Bar Clandestino, Paris; The Barking Dog,
Copenhagen; Sacapalabras, Oaxaca;
The Barking Dog, Copenhagen;
Tio's Cerveceria, Surry Hills*

TASTING
NOTES

5 SENTIDOS

El Destilado (see page 116), is a *mezcaleria* with an intriguing collection of deep, powerful, flooringly distinctive and highly recommended mezcals. These are sourced by young American proprietor Jason Cox and a few of them are now available to buy abroad. *Cinco Sentidos*, 'The Five Senses', are decked out with handsome artwork on the labels and are a real experience. Batches average only about two hundred litres (forty-four gallons) so, if you ever come across one, move quickly on it.

PAPALOTE

This is an *Agave potatorum* from Puebla, an area Jason's put a lot of time into exploring. It was made by Jose Luis Tobán Castilla in August 2016, fermented dry for three days and then for a further six in well water. It's distilled once to produce a fantastically perfumed, luscious and complex mezcal. Sweet plum notes in a gust of bonfire smoke, and liquorice on the tail.

SIERRA NEGRA

An *Agave americana* from Santa Catarina Albarradas, Oaxaca. This is a twelve-year-old Sierra Nevada plant, as the *americana* is sometimes known, ground by hand, fermented for a whopping fifteen days and distilled in clay pots by Alberto Martinez for a yield of two hundred litres (forty-four gallons). Soft as velvet and deep with layer after layer of fruity, earthy flavours.

AGAVE DE CORTES

At one o clock this morning in the otherwise deserted Calle Garcia Vigil of Oaxaca, a *mezcaleria*, packed into a cubby-hole of an old colonial row, was going off.

Heaving choruses of popular *canciones* and people from around the world came pouring out of the doorway. I was talking with a dashing Danish royal (rolling a joint) when the owner gave me his card. It read: 'Asis Cortes, sixth generation *mezcalero'*. The youngest in one of the longest-running Oaxacan *mezcalero* dynasties: the Family Cortes.

~

The family's roots are in Santiago Matatlán. There, their forefathers built a small *palenque* by a fork in one of the three rivers that once fed the town.

Visiting recently, we found two fermentation rock pits carved in a cliff head above the charred remains of a small earth oven. A moving experience. Far enough beyond the edge of town to feel the massive presence of ancient cliff walls, everything felt momentarily simple, timeless and innocent.

The modest but enterprising Casa Cortes company now has offices in Oaxaca City and from there they run a small oligarchy. All the bottles are produced by Renaldo Martinez and are made in one *palenque*, in Matatlán, five hundred yards from the original site by the river.

ESPADIN

This is fresh, bright, clean, with a pleasant splash of strong alcohol to the tongue that comes off like a gin. Nice…

…However, it was the **REPOSADO CON GUSANO** – I know! – that did it for me. A delicate affair: no cloying syrups and a gently soothing energy. The whole thing is permeated by the soft fungal hum of a tasty mushroom-like presence, which is the flavour of the worm. It reminds me of the Ven a Mi *reposado*, which is also from Matatlán, but sadly no longer available abroad.

Try and find this one. It's really delicious, and, with the combo of both worm and *reposado* (not just one, but two of the mezcal no-nos), it's a nice up-yours to the snobs.

ALIPÚS

Alipús offers beautifully produced, straightforward yet distinctive mezcals. The first three listed here are all *espadins* gathered from Oaxaca (in roughly a hundred-mile radius), but dramatically different. Don't be put off by the ubiquity of the brand. They're as good as it gets on the international market, a fine display of the possibilities of terroir.

SAN JUAN
Classic San Juan del Rio mezcal done perfectly. An abundance of sweet oils, smoke and an energetic lacing of fruits trailing into an inky finish. My personal fave in the range.

SAN BALTAZAR
Smoke just as a peripheral hint. Very clean, very fresh, but I've never been able to get past the striking flavour of cherry boiled sweets (hard candies). Though others find it practically perfect.

SANTA ANA
Largely herbal but with flowers, fruits and perfumes all gently swimming along in unctuous oils. Easy on the smoke, so as an introduction to the joys of mezcal, a good place to start.

SONORA
A *bacanora* (see page 61), distilled first in steel, then copper. Don Julián Urquijo uses *Agave pacifico* to deliver sweet berry fruits, nice oils, a tinge of smoke and another of boiled sweets (hard candy).

DURANGO
Classic *Agave durangensis*. Nutty, musty, sweet leathers, but light across the palate. Made in the Nombre de Dios *palenque* with its wood-and-copper alembic still.

DANGEROUS DON

I was surprised to learn that mezcal was being made in Mexico before the first coffee had been brewed there. The bean wasn't imported from the Dominican Islands until the eighteenth century! No doubt the idea of combining the two as an ultimate speed-ball *curado* was not long in coming. More recently, the combo became well known through the infusions of a Frenchman on the coast of Puerto Escondido, a mellow surf city with plenty of traffic from travellers, who often came away banging on about the joys of 'coffee mezcal'. This is how fellow Brit and *mezcalera* Thea Cumming came across it and she has found a great team to produce this: Mario Mendoza of Sin Piedad and *maestro* Don Celso, who works a perfect wonder here. Doubtless honouring the original recipe, he ramps it up a notch or two as, rather than using a random *espadin*, this is made with his own signature juice, which is top-notch. Miraculously, there's *espadin* galore in the final product, encompassing rich coffee tastes in oils and smoke. Then there's the buzz. Phenomenal.

DEL MAGUEY

Del Maguey is the foundation stone for mezcal as we know it outside Mexico. It is the grandfather clock against which all things in this, the first wave of mezcal international, can be measured.

This is not said casually. Few can argue with it, though many would wish to do so. The owner, Ron Cooper, is a man who courts controversy. A member of the West Coast art movement of the 1960s, he calls Ed Ruscha and the late Dennis Hopper close friends.

He has attitude and that is what has shaped, it can be argued, the course of mezcal as it is today. Had he not dug in his heels and known exactly what he wanted for the spirit back in the mid-1990s in the nascent moments of its current explosion, mezcal might have already been forced down the same industrial chutes as tequila.

~

Regardless of how one sees all this, you'll notice the bottles everywhere, bright green, emblazoned with terrific coloured drawings by the late Kenny Price, also a friend of Cooper's. For the last twenty years they have been a constant presence on back bars (and often in wells) around the world.

To pull that off has taken years of hard graft, concentration of will, supreme confidence and a true understanding of the spirit itself. I tip my hat to him.

And to these three bottles. They're crucial to the world of mezcal.

VIDA

Ubiquitous! And for good reason. It's classic and simple but with character, and priced so you can splash it about, as it should be: quaffed. How it's priced where it is is a well-guarded secret. We're told there is not a drop of water added. The spirit is 42% ABV. Miracle work. It's classic and simple, smooth, spicy and smoky with a bit of the old pot pourri.

CHICHICAPA

The Chichicapa by Don Faustino was the first bottle in the Del Maguey range. It comes from San Baltazar Chichicapam where the hills are steep and the challenges to the plants that grow there make for fantastically delicious mezcals. I have a soft spot for this one. Sweet and savoury, butterscotch and pineapple vibes. And smoke.

IBERICO

I'm not sure why I chose to review this bottle. It's a third distillation *pechuga* (see page 65) with a slab of Iberico ham in for the third round. It's all a bit luxurious and unaffordable to most of us, even if one can find it. But I'm glad I did. It's lean and clean and worth the special treat. A solid demonstration of creativity and skill.

DERRUMBES

One of the most rewarding ranges on the market, the product of the combined efforts of Venenosa's Esteban Garibi and Sergio Mendoza Garcia of Don Fulano. With this brand they achieve an equal measure of the sublime and slightly unusual, seeking out mezcals that represent a region, while possessing a rare flourish.

CHINO-ALTO
Made with the classic Michoacán materials: a Filipino still, subterranean fermentation – in pine wood tanks – and the signature glass *garrafónes* buried in earth. It uses *Agave cupreata* and *cenizo* plants (this *cenizo* being *americana oaxacaensis*), a nice twist on the classic; the two varietals combine to create a complex yet well-balanced mezcal. Vegetal, fruity, peppers and smoke.

SALMIANA
One of the few San Luis Potosían mezcals on the market, or even outside the region. Produced from the divine *Agave salmiana*, this expresses the chalk of its terroir clearly, as the giant nineteenth-century metal oven of the *palenque* is above ground, delivering a much less dominant smoke. A great place to start for those wishing to get into terroir and tradition, while going easy on bonfire vibes.

ESPADIN
Again, a wonderful flip on the familiar, this time in Oaxaca with the trusty *espadin*, but employing *pulque* in the fermentation: a delicious way of prompting the ambient yeasts. Coming in at a healthy 48%, this is big and bold with tons of detail and a long finish. Try it.

DON FULANO

A rare tequila range that is still made using an old-style double column still and alembic; intriguing, complex, not overpriced. Owner and connoisseur (he owns Derrumbes, opposite, as well) Sergio Mendoza Garcia has moved tequila to a better place, combining the best of both its pre-industrial past and modern accomplishments.

BLANCO
Made in Atotonilco where a lot of the most interesting tequilas that I've tried come from, this *blanco* is elegant and aromatic, with spices, citrus and a sweet agave note.

AÑEJO
Quite simply the finest *añejo* tequila that I've tasted. No added sweeteners or colourings or other weirdnesses of that sort get in between the spirit and the barrel. A complex recipe balancing different ages of spirits, ranging from two to five years, brings this home. A nice way to wrap up the day.

FUERTE
My kind of tequila: 50% ABV, so rich with lots of flavours to enjoy. Naturally. Spices and sweet agave amplified as they should be. And long. Recommended.

EL JOLGORIO

A *jolgorio* is a fiesta that revolves around giving and sharing of both gifts and culture. You arrive with something and receive in return. In this case we hand over a small fortune – these are not cheap mezcals – but I've always felt the exchange most worthwhile.

TEPAZTATE

Easily in the top ten of all mezcals I've tried, and in the top five of the branded bottles. I tasted it with a Swedish mixologist who brilliantly called out, 'Rainy highway!' I added, 'Listening to Joy Division.' It's moody but warm. A wet road, post-tropical deluge. Diesel. Tar from a hull. Sour ink and violets. Find this bottle.

MADRECUIXE

Like the complex, colourful images of its label, this bottle unfolds and folds again, slowly taking shape as an unforgettable mezcal. True to form, it is vegetal and – in this case – highly mineral. It's sit-down-in-the-armchair-and-contemplate time.

ARROQUEÑO

Carrying hints of the classic Miahuatlán profile: tropical fruits, bananas and pineapples. This is colourful stuff, with a calming effect given by the cool flavour of wet limestone.

ENMASCARADO

These *espadins*, made by Maestro Memo in Santiago Matatlán, are like the all-you-really-need kit bag of mezcal, nailing both ends of the spectrum with aplomb.

45

The house pour at La Clandestina in Mexico City (see page 215), Enmascarado 45 is the let's-go-dancing-it's-Saturday-night mezcal. Strangely light on its toes while delivering lots of flavours: toffee and lime, smoke and sweet agave.

54

Way more easy-going than you might expect for the highest ABV on the market. But definitely one to take your time over. Karla Moles, who bottles this, tells me the 45 is for celebrating while the 54 is for big decisions. I found my tasting notes the other day: 'wood-roasted peppers, olives, snuff and billiard baize. The resonating whoosh of a humidor. A force of nature. Rush matting, lovage and chewed leaves. Travelling.'

GEM & BOLT

There may be a touch of destiny surrounding Gem & Bolt mezcal. The brand's creators, AdrinAdrina and Elliot Coon — who embody a magical glamour that, in my eyes, crowns them a kind of Glimmer Twins of mezcal — had already long been a creative team under the G&B name when they were told of the ancient lore of mezcals' first roast. The story is set in a time of myth and the land of the ancients where, one dark night, a bolt of lightning struck the giant gem-shaped treasure of the agave, cooking it in an instant and — on the spot — instructing the four-leggeds and the early people how to live from its food, make *tepache* (see page 24) and, in time, mezcal.

In another case of it-was-always-going-to-be-this-way, they had begun playing with concoctions and preparations in their Oakland, California loft and makeshift bar room, marrying various 'medicines' with various mezcals, when they hit upon an especially winning combo of *espadin* infused with the Mayan love nut damiana, a seed understood to bear aphrodisiac qualities. Little did they know at the time, but this is an age-old recipe from mezcal country, used as a favourite *curado* for years.

'The two plants are lovers,' Adrina explains. And I don't doubt it for a minute. It is demonstrably amorous stuff. The sweetly botanical flavour, with a light, ashy smoke, has a glowing fire about it and, I've noticed, can produce the urge to hug a lot. All the better for the world we live in, now that it's bottled up, widely available and flying off shelves.

ILEGAL

Ilegal gets its name from a creative approach to customs, at border control and at the *palenque*.

His worldly patrons at the Café No Sé in Antigua Guatemala appreciated some proper hooch and owner, Jon Rexer, knew where to find it. Legend has it, Rexer made the thousand-mile run north to Oaxaca, where he met fourth-generation *mezcalero* Eric Hernandez and, one way or another, got what was needed back to his bar.

Meanwhile, Hernandez was himself playing with boundaries, having built a *horno* that gave off a super-light smoky taste while demnding far fewer brutal man hours. One among a number of breakthroughs that led to the hooch we now find on the shelves at our local offie.

An all-round creative affair.

JOVEN

For me, the *espadin*, coming in at 40%, is not something that I can get worked up about. The flavours are all present and correct, though I don't find it that dynamic. But try it and decide for yourself. It's not expensive or hard to find.

AÑEJO

Like other brands that work their mezcals around the 40% mark, Ilegal's juice seems better suited to *reposados*. If you like that kind of thing, then you'll be happy here. This has plenty of fruits and oils without overwhelming the spirit with treacles (blackstrap molasses), and allows a little agave to come through.

IN SÍTU

In Sítu, the Oaxacan *mezcaleria* (see page 118), is a gold mine of extraordinarily exquisite mezcals. If only the mezcals that proprietor, writer and mezcal touchstone, Ulises Torrentera, were bottling for the bar were available outside Mexico, there would be no room for doubt that mezcal is a king of spirits with all the possibility of wines. Sadly, as I go to press, we cannot get a single one… but that is soon to change, so don't despair.

JABALI

This, made from the *jabali* agave and overseen by master *mezcalero* Torrentera himself, will be first out of the gate. A masterpiece in balance with the overall effect on the light and uplifting side of things. Bright citrus vibes with woods and earth. I mean, if you can, just get it. The flavours I can describe… but the feeling, I cannot.

KOCH

Koch – pronounced with a 'tch' sound on the end, in case you were wondering – is a strong brand with a big range and some very elegant design work.

ESPADIN

One of the nicest *espadins* in the game. Plenty of classic aromas on the nose – peats and smoke and cooked agave – but with a neat, sweet stone (pit) fruit note on the finish, *también*. Just ideal stuff. All these flavours, merely hinted at, leap to life on the tongue, where it also reveals an especially luxurious texture, strangely rounded, as if there were a bubble – a hemispherical lens – of sweet oils gathered there.

LUMBRE

The *lumbre* is an indigenous Oaxaqueño agave that has escaped classification. Here, in the hands of producer Pedro Hernández, it's showing us a warming plum note, modest smoke and a tight and even balance.

ENSAMBLE

Like the brand's *espadin*, their *ensamble* is one of the signature mezcals for the range. Sought after for its smooth complexity, it's a mezcal to contemplate and take time over. Vanillas meet spices meet fruits meet the unmistakable bite of the various agaves that go into it: the *espadin*; the *cirial* and *tobasiche* (both types of *karwinskii*); and the perfumed *tobalá*.

LA VENENOSA

A truly sterling range of *raicillas* created by the leading pioneer of the branded category, Esteban Morales of Guadalajara, Jalisco. As we know (see page 59), *raicilla* falls beneath the shadow of the tequila giants and scatters productions where there is a toe-hold. These three *raicillas* come from quite different regions and deliver, true to the spirit's style, super-radical results.

SUR DE JALISCO

La Sur is an *espadin* (of sorts) grown at four thousand feet above sea level. It's roasted in earth pit ovens and distilled in clay pots by *maestro* Macario Partida in the village of Zapotitlán de Vadillo. With that combo you won't go wrong... but get ready, because *raicillas* pack the funk. In this case, among delicious fruits, smokes and woods, is rubber. It sounds odd, but it's great in the mix. Though you might only go for one of an evening.

COSTA DE JALISCO

Next we go to the coast where *maestro* Don Alberto Hernández roasts *Agave rhodacantha* with a local *espadin* in stone ovens before distilling Filipino-style in a tree trunk. And yes, masses of funk again. Rubber returns, this time with lemon and menthol, pepper and aniseed. This is why we love *raicillas*. Proper, eccentric good stuff.

SIERRA OCCIDENTAL DE JALISCO

Finally we go to my favourite. I truly love this mezcal. Tons of stewed prunes (dried plums) – I can't bear to eat them, but I love the flavour here! – an incredible sweet-and-sour play with spices and minerals. If you want to try something out there but totally together, I recommend it.

LÁGRIMAS DE DOLORES

The seventeenth-century Hacienda Dolores, 'mansion of sadness', houses this *viñata*. A further blessing comes in the form of the abundance of wild, unusual agaves that proliferate there. Other mezcals I've tasted by the *viñata* are equally good, but brutally are made of varieties that only grow at certain altitudes, and these remote locations have been commandeered for the use of narcos, which makes harvesting sketchy… to say the least.

JOVEN 45%

A *cenizo*, the colloquial name for *Agave durangensis*, this shows a strong sweet tobacco and fungal musk that appears on the nose, blossoming into prunes (dried plums) and figs and sour-wet soils and woods on the tongue.

AÑEJO

Delicate and woody, amplifying the natural aromas of the *cenizo* itself. A little stronger in alcohol on the nose than I was expecting from its 40.5%, but room for some subtleties of vanilla. No cloying syrups here, thanks to the use of new barrels. Retaining great freshness and bestowing a lovely warming feeling and a nice easiness on the mind.

I'GOK

The jewel in the crown, the fantastic (by name and nature) I'Gok. A local form of the *Agave durangensis* and, in the hands of *maestra* Fabiola Ávila Valenzuela, the best example of why we really don't need *reposados*. Soft, sweet, soothing warmth. Nutty – almond on the nose, walnut on the tongue – and a little lactic, in the realm of yogurt. All elegantly complemented by leather. It may sound odd, but it's not. I can't recommend it highly enough.

LOS CABRONES

The legend of Los Cabrones is not known by many. Word is of a masterful epicurean and a heroic spear fisherman who ventured to the mountains above Monterrey and found a village that, left to its own devices, had developed an unusual spirit. To say the least.

DESTILADO DE PULQUE

To make one hundred and twenty litres (twenty-six gallons) of this, eight hundred litres (one hundred and seventy-six gallons) of *agua miel* (see page 22) is needed. *Eight hundred litres*. And the trick is to keep it all fermenting at the right rate, so that once it becomes *pulque* you're ready to distil again... and on and on you go – twice round! – until it comes out, your one hundred and fifty bottles, as a very unusual form of mezcal.

Unusual and phenomenally good. In fact, an unforgettable experience. With sweet, delicate flavours and a cooling sensation on the tongue. Like a lightly chalky pink lemonade with the hints of the once raw sap. Let me know if you find it. The *Animal Chin* of mezcal.

LOS DANZANTES

Los Danzantes are infamous figures – throwing shapes – carved in relief on to the temple walls of Monte Alban, the ancient Zapotec city over Oaxaca. Similarly, the company, Los Danzantes, has carved itself into the history of mezcal. At its head are twins Jaime and Gustavo – gifted with the ability to fathom the cultural context of mezcal while navigating the business terrain – and their partner, Hugo D'Acosta, a wine-maker. In the 1990s, Jaime and Gustavo opened a restaurant in Mexico City. When asked to suggest a drinks menu, Hugo offered what was at the time booming: tequila. But forays into the region had not felt inspiring, so they turned South, on a hunch, to Oaxaca. They poked about and, in San Juan del Rio, met a chap named Rodolfo Juan Juarez who poured them a mezcal that would change the course of the culture's history. It inspired a company that would bring the undiscovered country of mezcal to the outside world. It was more or less the beginning of mezcal as we know it.

Their bottles are now found in eighteen countries yet how the *mezcaleros* work, the *agaveros* they buy from and the way that they harvest, nothing's changed. An extraordinary feat and a shining example of how it can be done.

ESPADIN

Cool, bright and rounded. Classic in its flavour profiles, but definitely not ordinary, this has light herb notes, a balanced amount of smoke and nice spices.

REPOSADO

This one is heavy on the syrup, with hints of corn, an aged spirit that moves towards a brandy in expression. Good if you like that sort of thing.

AÑEJO

Goes further in the Old World direction and wins. Super-thick and intense in its flavours. I forget there's agave in there at all, but I don't mind. A giant pineapple note and all the woods and tannins make it enjoyable.

LOS SIETE MISTERIOS

The mezcals of *Los Siete Misterios* – 'The Seven Mysteries' – are nectar direct from the source. That source being the most rudimentary and prized technique of clay-pot still productions. Two brothers, Julio and Eduardo Mestre, quickly concluded, when they undertook to form their own brand in 2010, that they had no choice but to bring to the world the best they had tried… those were a collection of seven plants from the hills of Sola de Vega, where clay-pot production is the tradition.

ESPADIN

Text-book mezcal masterpiece. Practically beyond description for its complexity, yet in universal balance. Spices, celery, stone (pit) fruits, wisps of smoke and herbs. One of the finest clay-pot *espadins* on the market.

TOBALÁ

The *tobalá* batch I'm familiar with from these guys is a 2013. It had a lot of lemon and was bright and well-made, though I wasn't able to drink a lot of it in one sitting. I believe there's a 2016 on the market now and I have no doubt it would be worthwhile seeking it out.

DOBA-YEJ

The anomaly in the range, distilled in copper in Matatlán (by the incomparable Don Celso, who makes a number of most wonderful mezcals also reviewed in this book). As the yield is higher than clay-pot, the bottle is more affordable and stands as the entry level for the brand. A pretty glamorous place to start. Really wonderful mezcal. Tobaccos, spices, clean, oily and long. Love it.

MARCA NEGRA

From the most remote place I've been. We'd driven hours to get there, from valley floor to impossible mountain passes, to reach a thriving oasis. Palms lined a river and blue-and-green agave shone all about. In this mezcal village of two hundred souls, the entire community gathers around two earth ovens, six *tiñas* and two stills to make some of the finest mezcals on the market.

ESPADIN

Remarkably refreshing for a 51% ABV. There's a subtle minty note that brings that out, doubtless combined with all that alcohol on the tongue. Broad, wide, long and sweet and complex. A real sit-back-and-contemplate mezcal.

TOBALÁ

Grassy and smoky and not what I'd expect from a perfumed *tobalá*, but delicious nonetheless. Again massively powerful, weighing in at a hefty 52% ABV. I do wonder if that's a bit high for the flavours but, allowed to rest for a while after opening, this makes for a well-priced, satisfying *silvestre*.

METEORO

Great fun and great mezcal, Meteoro brings to the market something delicious, legit and affordable. The hooch is *espadin* from San Luis Del Rio, classic sweet smoke, peats and cooked agave whipped up in copper alembics. All 100% trad. As close as you'll get to out-of-this-world for the buck.

MEXCAL
BURRITO FIESTERO

A *fiestero* is a party animal. And a *burrito* is a burrito. Or a tiny, adorable donkey. Either way, the idea is cute festive abandon. Which is probably the best way to approach this lightweight party-slugger as, at 40% ABV, you're not in it for the contemplation. Though it is a tad unusual to get such mainstream mezcal from wild *Agave durangensis*, or *maguey cenizo*. Steel-pot stills and earth oven production give this bottle a little bit of everything: smoke, flowers and cooked agave. I'd love to try this at 47%.

MEZCAL GIN

There are a few of these mezcal gins on the market now... and why not? The possibilities are endless. Mezcal is distilled, then infused with aromatic herbs and spices – in this case the classic European botanicals for gin of juniper and coriander seed as well as Mexican native varieties – then distilled for a second time.

This one does surprisingly more than the simple name would suggest, going the extra mile by working with a *cenizo* base, then adding native Mexican aromatics of ancho chilli (chile), hibiscus, lemongrass and avocado leaves into the mix. Chin chin!

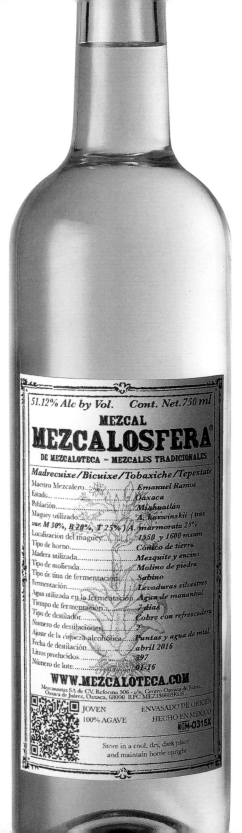

MEZCALOSFERA

The mezcals of Mezcaloteca in Oaxaca (see page 122) have been a yardstick of quality since the bar opened in 2010. At last, Marco and Silvia have prepared bottles to send out into the beyond under the name Mezcalosfera (mezcal meets the *atmosfera*) and we are not disappointed.

So far, there have been three batches of about four hundred litres (eighty-eight gallons) each. This is the third and I cannot recommend it highly enough. It really is something you should do all you can to track down and eke out for as long as you possibly can. It's an ensemble of different types of agave: *madrecuixe*, *bicuixe*, *tobaxiche* and *tepaxtate*, as it's spelled locally in Miahuatlán, where *maestro* Emanuel Ramos makes his spirits. Flavour-wise, I found the tropical fruits and plantain vibes I often get from the finer mezcals from the region, along with nice smokes and cooked agave, of course. But find out what it tastes like for yourself.

MEZONTE

Now, there are mezcals, and then there's mezcals. That is to say, there are levels. I used to think one mezcal, made according to the tradition, by hand, would always serve a purpose and have its place and none could really be considered better than others. What does that even mean, 'better'? But I've come to learn over time.

Mezonte mezcals roll around on those upper realms where things go from great to simply other-wordly and words no longer really suffice. The mad, eccentric opposites that are somehow complementary — and the drama that they usher to the senses — are surprising and wonderful and tricky to explain.

At a push I would say that they are typically stinky and musty and lactic and fungal and foul with some brilliant sweet, delicious opposite that you cling to and swing about on until it lets you out easy. They're all tiny batches — this *Amarillo y Verde* by Manuel Ramos is only sixty litres (thirteen gallons) — and hard to get. Find 'em.

MI CHINGÓN

Karl Lenin wasn't in it for the money. A Mexican documentary movie-maker with a fateful name, he only wanted to buy twenty litres (four gallons) for mates and himself. But mezcal has a way of making its own kind of sense, especially in the rural heart of a place like Guerrero. Lenin left with four hundred litres (eighty-eight gallons) instead, and a deal penned on the back of a napkin. He decided to call his project *Mi Chingón*, meaning, more or less, 'my homey', 'my mate'... or 'the devil'.

~

Karl found himself getting involved in the community. He met a botanist who recommended reforestation. That, as an idea, made much more sense than trying to sweat the communal *palenque* to try and turn a profit. He and the botanist discovered endemic agaves that were on the verge of extinction and plants that used to be part of the ecosystem... and reintegrated them. Other farmers began to do it, too. The landscape started changing. Changing back. Wildlife, it was noticed, was returning. The village felt revitalized. Lenin sat on the community board. He bought two bulls and raised money for a new church roof. The mezcal, this rich and luscious mezcal, that he was occasionally bottling up and making mellow deals over back in Mexico City, had become a happy by-product of his communal work. Just as it had always been done in the past. Perhaps as it was always meant to be. Lenin, living up to his name.

~

I was given a bottle made from **AGAVE CUPREATA** a few years back and it only came out on the most special occasions. If you find some of this 52% ABV spirit, expect a slowly revealed deep complexity. Elegant sweet vanilla yogurt with a grapefruit blush, softly dissolving into spice and liquorice, classic *cupreata* wet tobaccos and oils.

Just banging.

NUESTRA SOLEDAD

The Nuestra Soledad range is Oaxaqueño craft-production *espadíns* put together by the Cortes family (see page 139) that also bring us El Jolgorio (see page 146). They point out: first, that tasting this range is an instructive way of fathoming the characteristics of terroir and regional production styles, as the plant (unlike in the El Jolgorio range) remains the same; and second, that mezcal heals the Mexican soul, so deftly described in *The Labyrinth of Solitude* by Octavio Paz, from which they draw the name – 'Our Loneliness' – a thing that mezcal can heal. I agree with both of those arguments.

ZOQUITLÁN

A peculiar and evocative combination of rubber and leather on the nose, followed by blueberry jam, flowers and boiled sweets (hard candies) on the tongue. This is made within a stone's throw of the exemplary Rey Campero *palenque* and the Vago HQ, where the noble strong-man of mezcal, Aquilino, makes his terrific 'juice'.

EJUTLA

This is from a wonderful neck of the mezcal wood: El Campañero, Ejutla, an hour or two from Oaxaca City. Here, the tradition is to make mezcals using only single distillation stills or *refrescadoras*. The process brings the mezcals in strong, rich and remarkably delicious. Expect complex flavours here, including buttercups, diesel and *tepache* (see page 80), bright with a long finish.

PAPADIABLO

Papadiablo: the Pope and the Devil. Two opposing forces, yin and yang. On a night out, it could go either way. But, as the best mezcals should, it stays in balance.

ESPADIN

Papadiablo is made in the dry and dusty mountains of Miahuatlán, South of Oaxaca City. The landscape is tough and forbidding, as are the people. Waltzing in with a smile and a handshake won't get you anywhere. It takes time to get to know someone. And there are a lot of people who want to get to know *maestro* Don Beto Ortiz. To shake the gifted *mano*.

His *espadin* is so unique it's as if it were another kind of drink all of its own. The flavours, delicate, sweet stone (pit) fruits and a lactic touch, come with an ever-so-slightly effervescent fizz. This is mezcal of the highest quality.

ESPECIAL

In a *Desert Island Discs* radio show scenario where you're lost at sea and could only have one mezcal for the rest of time, which would it be? For me, without hesitation, it would be Don Beto Ortiz's Papadiablo Especial. Something in the balance of the alcohol and the plants: *madrecuixe, tobasiche, mexicano* and *espadin*. Or, perhaps, the truly *especial* benediction performed over every batch. I won't try to describe the flavours, only someone once put it like this: a long chord played on a baby grand by a large hand in a scarlet room, smoke, and the clinking of glasses.

PATRÓN

My soft spot for Patrón tequila comes from all those hilarious rap videos that the company sponsored in the 1990s, when it was considered the height of swagger to bang bottles with your posse on yachts circling the New York harbour.

SILVER

I don't find the drink itself to be nearly so much fun, but there are some sterling traditional techniques employed in production – namely the use of a *tahona* and a *mamposteria* oven – so, though when sipped I find the flavours a little sharp, I'm happy to choose it for my mixer in an ice-cold margarita.

XO CAFÉ

I must admit that I was surprised by how much I took to this drink. I also confess that I had rather meanly selected it for review solely against which to highlight the outstanding qualities of Dangerous Don (see page 141). Here, let me make amends. This stuff, taken at face value and simply as the sum of its parts – a bunch of industrial tequila softened out with a splash of filtered coffee and flavourings – is good fun. A little boozy aperitif that would probably work pretty well in cocktails, too.

PESCADOR DE SUEÑOS

'Mezcal changed my life.' It's uncanny how often you hear this. I say it myself. But it's more unexpected coming from Juan Carlos — better known as *Tio Pesco*, 'the fisherman of dreams' — whose background as an astute and successful businessman makes such cosmic-speak sound especially unusual.

~

He had simply marked the mezcal trade as a smart investment and decided to get involved. But mezcal is full of surprises and he tells me, with disbelief, how dramatically the decision affected the entire outlook and course of his life. 'I am a muse of the agave,' he assures me. What happened is, as he became more immersed in the culture of the plant, he experienced a kind of awakening. Getting to know the *mezcaleros* and *campesinos* and their families, all living in relation to the long life cycles of the agave and the earth, worked on him like a kind of chiropractic, realigning his approach to business, family, time, money... all of it. Including his relationship with, or how he thought about, the natural world.

~

He was the first person I heard say out loud what I'd been intuiting for some time. That the different species of agave, and so the different mezcals that we have, impart different energies, different moods.

Yes, I know — esoteric stuff, cosmic debris — which is why he embarked on a mission to prove his theory by mapping chemical compounds from the plants to neural patterns in our brains that create emotional responses in our bodies. Extensive research, developing medicines with homeopathic doctors in Germany, and with the medical board of Mexico. He clearly feels he's on to something.

~

As a brand, his Pescador de Sueños is all wild agaves and fancy bottling, while Aprendiz, at 40% ABV, is an introductory-level mezcal.

In the Pescador de Sueños range, the various mezcals, made from various plants, list their ascribed energies and what to expect from imbibing them. The **COYOTE** is said to 'lead you to an experience of introspection' and the **CUISHE** to the 'sexual domain', while the **TOBALÁ** is said to give 'a sense of accomplishment'. This, when spelled out, can sound all a bit treacherous but, as they all taste incredible, it's a lot of fun testing the theory.

I sat in a bar last night where Juan Carlos was giving a tasting. He had a great technique for walking us through it. He took Aprendiz **ESPADIN**, the Aprendiz **ESPADIN-TEPAZTATE** ensemble, then the Pescador de Sueños **TEPAZTATE**, lined them up, and we walked the stepping stones out, from the shallow waters of the 40% ABV *espadin* into the deep ocean *tepaztate* and the big game.

The success of this class hinged on us liking the 40% *espadin* in the first place. Luckily, for a mezcal that low in ABV, it's very, very tasty. A little smoke, a little fruit, a touch of tobacco. Just enough of each.

PIERDE ALMAS

Pierde Almas mezcals are, like their founder and his artwork – Jonathan Barbieri paints with oils – strong, clear, subtle and complex. They're also of a distinct style. In a blind tasting, I'd find it easier to call a Pierde Almas mezcal than I might any other brand. There's a direct power and a seemingly endless depth to each of them. Remarkably, with the new 40% ABV Puritita Verda offering, too. Making mezcal is a creative act and open to experimentation by its nature. Jonathan, an artist and master distiller, can't help but seize on that. The Conejo and the Botanica +9 are masterful creations made by someone playing with the medium and the materials.

ESPADIN

It seems so obvious now but, at the time – 2004 – it was a breakthrough when Pierde Almas decided to distinguish their mezcals by labelling the name of the plants on each bottle. It began with the *espadin*, a delicious, silk-and-velvet bouquet of smoke and chocolate with savoury spices. And properly delivered in the 48–51% ABV range for genuine mezcal flavour.

CONEJO

A *pechuga*, using 'the saddle of a wild cotton tail rabbit' with all the fruits there at the *palenque*. The results are simply remarkable. A savoury hint balancing the berries and mint; unforgettable and worth the price tag.

BOTANICA +9

I love the taste of gins, being British after all, but if I can replace that grain spirit with agave spirit, why hesitate? Not only does it get us around the maudlin moods, the deep oily Pierde Almas *espadin* is the ultimate vehicle for carrying forth the aromatic contingent of incredible spices, sourced in Mexico. As in cooking, oils carry the flavour and this gin becomes magnified to the power of... 9? Highly recommended. Good fun.

LA PURITITA VERDA

A new addition to the PA fold, built to splash about and mix in cocktails, this holds its own as a sipper all the same. Made in San Juan del Rio, where so many of the classics are, it has all the earth and smoke and sweet taste of *espadin* you'd expect.

QUIQUIRIQUI

The first time I heard about The QuiQuiRiQui girls was from friends in Mexico City who had just sent them UK-bound on a quest to wake the world and show them how wonderful and exciting life can be when you 'Just add mezcal!' They gave me their number.

~

I called. Jen picked up, mid-mouthful and swearing madly and loudly, the foulest language I'd heard since school. It was fantastic. We met at the pub. They said they were going to open a bar. They did. They're like that. I stocked them. We moved a lot of good hooch through that place in its brief window of existence. Melanie told me they had to sweep up glass an inch deep every morning before opening up again for another go. It was wild. From that auspicious start rose Britain's first mezcal brand. Hats off. Melanie works hard to make these great mezcals financially viable. She's bringing mezcal to the people in the way that it was brought to her. Flowing. And with love. Two bottles. Two expressions. Nice and simple. Both *espadins*.

SANTIAGO MATATLÁN
A classic Matatlán mezcal with delicious roast agave at the heart of it.

SAN JUAN DEL RIO
Exclusive to the brand and producing in batches of six hundred litres (one hundred and thirty-two gallons), keeping a nice and tight production quality and giving us some great citrus and floral vibes with our green agave flavours while they're at it.

REAL MINERO

The Mendoza family oversee every aspect, from production to shelf. They also make only clay-pot mezcals, as is traditional to Santa Catarina Minas, Oaxaca, where they live. The combination of clay-pot — historically, the Southern rural way — and a family-run business makes these mezcals authentic to the nth degree. And they are exquisite.

LARGO
Clay-pot mezcals are like photos with an infinite depth of pixillation, as compared to a snap taken on your phone. The *largo* — a long-leaved form of *karwinskii* unique to Santa Catarina — in this expression carries an exotic savoury hint with pomace fruits.

BARRIL
Clay-pot mezcals tend to improve with time. When I first opened this *barril* — a particularly rotund sub-species of the *karwinskii* (hence the nickname 'barrel') — I found it sharp, fresh, sour like a freshly cut plant. Returning to the bottle two years later, soft notes of cocoa and caramel had created a much deeper, multi-faceted experience.

PECHUGA
I was lucky and found two batches of this at the Brooklyn spot, Madre, both made by the late, great Lorenzo Angeles Mendoza, one in 2014 and t'other in 2015 and, most likely, using the same recipe, to which I'm partly privy, confirmed on the nose (especially of the 2014): mandarins and nuts with, I found, a subtle gel of yogurt. The combination is so winning I could have easily spent the rest of that rainy Sunday huffing on my *copita*. It was even more engrossing on the palate. The velvet, cream, the sheer luxury… and I'm not a fan of *pechugas*. The 2015 was more herbaceous — rosemary and thyme — with cocoa and coffee and tobacco to close. Quite another thing, which is why Real Minero is probably the only brand where vintages truly count. Don Mendoza only ever responded to the moment during his entire impeccable career.

SIN PIEDAD

Sin Piedad – 'without piety' – is flawless. Broad, robust, powerful and delicious. It is an *espadín* made in Santiago Matatlán, though *maestro* Don Celso manages to extrapolate a richness and depth that might suggest it was from deep in the mountains. Expect a merciful degree of fine smoke, fruit and sweet cooked agave flavours. Recommended.

SOMBRA

A big brand, the second biggest seller in the United States and climbing fast. The owners are focused. There's – cleverly – only one bottle in the range. It used to be made out in San Juan del Rio and was the best bang for your buck, but they've moved now into Santiago Matatlán and built a huge high-tech *palenque* that manages to pump out two hundred thousand litres (forty-four thousand gallons) a year. It's mezcal produced on a mass scale.

The stuff tastes OK. Classic flavours – smoke and all that – but what I like is that it knows what it is and doesn't pretend to be anything else. It's not trying to tell you it's artisanal. It's agave and it's cheap and it has a cheesy gang-tat logo. It does just enough of the traditional and the tech to make it taste fine and make money. It's the mezcal equivalent of a high-end tequila. Which says something about both mezcal and tequila.

SOTOL POR SIEMPRE

'Sotol Forever': a wonderful thought. And not entirely out of the question as, unlike the agave, when harvested correctly (neatly between the root and the *piña*), the sotol plant will grow back in its entirety to be potentially harvested for ever more.

The makers of this, what I consider to be an especially good agave spirit, are a family that have been producing *sotoles* for six generations. The eldest working soul in the outfit today is 73 years old. His name is Manuel Mendez Ponce and he was taught by real-life outlaw and master distiller Don Cuco (see page 65), starting work with him when he was 13.

The mezcal he's had a hand in making is quick with oils and perfumed. Dry flowers and stone (pit) fruits and citrus vibes wrapped in a gentle smoke. The smoke is really just gracing the spirit, as the practice at the Janos *vintaña* is to add around eighty litres (eighteen gallons) of water to the earth oven once the *piñas* are loaded, to steam the plants as they roast.

TAPATIO

When I first tried to spread the good word on mezcal in London, I often met people who said that tequila was nicer. I worried for them. But Tapatio was a tequila I liked.

BLANCO
I've visited Arandas where it's made; this drink is as feisty as the people. It's sharp, sheer and citrusy: it tastes like tequila… in a good way.

110
This ramps that up to 55% ABV. Pretty ballsy for a semi-industrial spirit and, as a stiff drink to wrap up a meal, it could be useful. But when compared with mezcals of the same strength, it comes off like a bit of a brawler, while the mezcal sits like a Zen monk.

TEQUILA OCHO

These tequilas are great mezcals, in part because they taste close to the earth – natural – and significantly because each bottle is based on its terroir. Inspired by visits to the Burgundy region of France, aficionado Tomas Estes teamed up with master distiller Don Carlos Camarena to make the first tequila that designates not only the year it was made, but the portion of the estate from which the agaves were harvested. It is the first genuine vintage in the category and each batch is pronouncedly different.

LA MAGUEYER
This is from the field we drew up to on our visit to the distillery. We'd taken the wrong turn and wound up on this little grey-soil lane immersed in blue agave peppered with strange trees. This translated into mints and mangoes and a nice high note of zesty lime.

LA LATILLA
From a considerably higher plane of the land and surrounded by oaks and pine, this was much more chalky and mineral, though still with a nice freshness accented by flavours of limes and grasses.

PUERTA DEL AIRE
Not far from the Rancho La Latilla, but strikingly other, with brown sugars and coffee, and spices showing on the palate.

TIER

A new range of decent mezcals with a website seemingly designed to appeal to nine-year-olds. But if you're able to get past the distracting graphics, you can find some tasty hooch. Hailing from Miahuatlán de Porfirio Diaz, there's a number of offerings: a *tepaztate*, an *ensamble* and here, an *espadin*. Coming in at 47% ABV, it's perfectly presentable. A little smoke and lots of that tropical fruity signature flavour of the region.

TOSBA

One Christmas Eve, my daughter and I swayed in procession through a tiny, remote village in the highlands of North Oaxaca. Fireworks detonated as glowing effigies of Joseph and Mary were held aloft and a man passed through the crowd, pouring shots of a ripping mezcal made by a young *maestro* called Edgar Gonzalez-Ramirez.

Edgar's story is incredible, as are the mezcals he makes here in San Cristóbal Lachirioag and calls Tosba, meaning 'ours'.

Edgar, like all the young men from the village, had gone North for work. Mezcal production in his region, though once a part of village life, had faded with the constant exodus and become a distant memory of which he'd never heard. Somehow, however, while staring at a TV in California, he experienced a genuine eureka moment and realized what possibilities his people had as a community back home. He returned having no idea of how to do it, but knowing he would make mezcal. It was 2004. Everyone thought he was mad.

It's now 2017 and Edgar's mezcals are celebrated wherever they can be found. Not only was he right – mezcal can give young men in his region an honest living – but they can be made well and to taste very differently from others.

In Zapoteco, where the village lies, it's gloriously hot and humid in the day, but by night it's cold. The place is a strange mix of alpine forest and jungle. Hearts of palm and banana trees grow alongside old oaks and raspberry bushes. In among this flourish huge unidentified variants of the *espadin* and *karwinskii*, among others. They have flavours all of their own.

ESPADIN

Unforgettable. Clean, green, bundled in dense oils and sugars. It reminds me of a *pechuga* and how cake-like the sugars become from the third distillation. But without the eccentricity of a *pechuga*, instead, this has an elegant simplicity.

PECHUGA

Remarkably, the least *pechuga*-esque *pechuga* I know. Not overly complex or kitsch, very fresh and green with wonderful subtleties. I've not tried it in three months and I can remember it perfectly. The sign of a great mezcal.

UNION

Union, a brand with big aspirations and the Diagio financial backing to match, now offers two mezcals.

EL VIEJO

In keeping with the trend, this is a 'single-village' *espadin / tobalá* from San Baltazar Guelavila, a place that produces the quintessential *espadins*. The *tobalá* lends a delicate perfumed touch to the well-balanced classic *espadin* profile. Viejo may refer to the time the *tobalá* takes to grow, but also to this offering being genuinely artisanal, of an old custom and recipe.

UNO

The *joven*, the entry level and signature of the brand, comes in both 38% and 40%, depending on the country you're in and its tax brackets. It must be said that the dollar is the bottom line here. Though attention is given to working with producers that are in roughly similar environments, it is only to create a uniform flavour. Artisanal in the true sense, this is not. Flavour-wise, it does the trick, but is not as good as El Viejo.

VAGO

There's a remote surf break along the Oaxacan Coast. People drift here to the beach and, rootless, they live off the land. *Vago*, as in 'vagrant', however, has a definite sense of place.

Judah and Dylan, young Americans chasing waves, found a life in mezcal following their dreams, and now call Zoquitlán and the *palenque* of strapping *maestro* Aquilino García López, home.

The company policy is simple – defer to the *maestro* – and, as such, we get an 100% pure expression of the region's deep mezcal style. The system works so well, the family could afford to bring their son home from Florida to join them.

ESPADIN

A perfect example of Oaxaqueño mezcal power and the flavours of remote Zoquitlán. Deep, viscous oils carrying citrus, pine and caramels. A nice high ABV. Proper mezcal.

ELOTE

Nothing more Mexican than corn. And though it doesn't sound right, it tastes amazing when roasted kernels grown on the land are put in for the third distillation. It's subtle but evocative. You connect with the land. I recommend.

BIEN PICADO

Bien picado means 'well picked over', and here refers to the agave standing for years beyond harvest time gathering weird flavours from the funk and decay of exposure. Resisting the urge to harvest sooner is rare, as are these bottles. This was a batch of two hundred, the entirety of which was sold in one go to the Texan *mezcaleria*, The Pastry War.

This kind of deal, exporting a whole batch abroad to one destination, be it bar, restaurant or distributor, is a new and super-effective way that some brands (Wahaka is another to watch here) are managing to get small-batch – which is, after all, the purest expression – mezcals out into the foreign markets. Bravo!

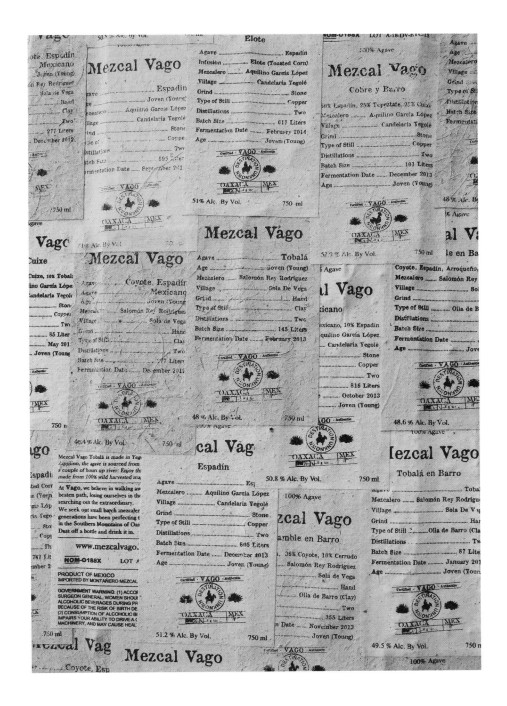

VIEJO INDECENTE

Mezcal is not polite. It doesn't seek anyone's approval. It knows how to let rip and, unlike its smoke-free cousin, is happily indecent. *Viejo Indecente*, or the 'Indecent Old Man', is a vigorous mezcal but also has no smoke.

~

Miahuatlán, where the VI *palenque* lies, has too few trees to keep roasting in an earth-pit oven sustainably. So the company bought a *mamposteria*, a stone mason oven that cooks slowly with steam, and makes lively mezcals that are steamed instead.

MADRECUICHE

Personally, I like a bit of smoke. With this mezcal, however, I didn't even notice its absence. There are so many other great things going on. I was sitting in a garden in Oaxaca, listening to Gilberto Gil, as the cup was passed to me.

The aromas were so plentiful, I literally looked round to see what was emanating such a potent scent. I've never experienced anything quite like it. I took it to the palate and, wonderfully, the thick, round notes of the sax solo from 'Girl from Ipanema' struck up as I sipped, lifting the mezcal notes with it. Memorable. Free of the smokiness, the fruity, herbal flavours of the *karwinskii* balloon out. It's a wonderful drink.

ESPADIN

Clean and bright. What tequila is going to taste like when the industry gets more daring.

COCKTAILS

RITUAL UNION

Gemma Terry, Ojo Rojo
Bournemouth, UK

VERDITA

Pineapple is the sweet, fruity base with green (bell) pepper adding a savoury lick and a vibrant green colour and flavour. This is enhanced by the mint for freshness and coriander (cilantro) for aroma. Green chilli (chile) is the spice and lime freshens it all up. Zesty, light, herbal and spicy. Gemma says, 'We call the addition of *verdita* or *sangrita* alongside our mezcal a "ritual union".'

GLASS: SHOT, ABOUT 100ML (3½fl oz)
about ½ pineapple, peeled and chopped
1 green (bell) pepper, deseeded and chopped
1 green chilli (chile), chopped,
    plus 1 to garnish (optional)
handful of coriander (cilantro) and
    mint leaves
1 lime

Run all the ingredients though a juicer. Serve with a green chilli, if you like.

SANGRITA

This is rich, sweet and spicy, with the red (bell) pepper adding a sweet vegetal note. Aim for a medium heat and serve alongside a large pouring of top-notch mezcal.

GLASS: SHOT, ABOUT 100ML (3½fl oz)
3 oranges
handful of strawberries, hulled
1 red chilli (chile), chopped, plus a chilli
    (chile) slice, to garnish (optional)
1 red (bell) pepper, deseeded and chopped
cayenne pepper
ancho chilli (chile) powder
pomegranate molasses
lemon juice

Juice the oranges, strawberries, fresh red chilli (chile) and red (bell) pepper, then season with all the other ingredients to taste. The cayenne pepper and the ancho chilli (chile) powder add heat and smoke, the pomegranate molasses a tangy sweet-sour undertone, while the lemon juice lifts all the other flavours. Garnish with the slice of chilli (chile), if you like.

[see previous page for recipe images]

SNAP OUT OF IT

Gemma Terry, Ojo Rojo
Bournemouth, UK

Fortaleza *blanco* is a peppery, spicy tequila with an inviting vegetal complexity. To complement this style here, we hone in on those vibrant green notes we often find in *blanco* tequilas.

GLASS: COUPE

7 sugar snap peas, plus more to garnish
50ml (1¾fl oz) Fortaleza *blanco* tequila
25ml (scant 1fl oz) lime juice
15ml (½fl oz) pure agave nectar
4 drops of celery shrub
2 spritzes of Fernet Branca

Muddle the sugar snaps in a cocktail shaker, add all the other ingredients except the Fernet, shake, then fine-strain into an ice-cold coupe and spritz with the Fernet. Garnish with a split sugar snap pea to make it memorable.

INSTANT CRUSH

Alex Kratena, P(our) Foundation
London, UK

GLASS: CERAMIC BOWL
20ml (¾fl oz) Del Maguey Chichicapa
20ml (¾fl oz) Tequila Ocho *blanco*
20ml (¾fl oz) fino sherry
25ml (scant 1fl oz) Melon & Cucumber Water
    (see right)
4 coriander (cilantro) leaves
1 tbsp lemon juice
2 tsp pure agave nectar
chorizo, to serve

For the rim of the glass
caster (superfine) sugar
sea salt
freshly ground Timur or Szechuan pepper

Mix together all the ingredients for the rim of the glass in a saucer. Wet the rim of a glass, or ideally a ceramic *copita*, by placing it upside down into a saucer of water, then into the rim ingredients, to get an evenly coated edge.

Place all the ingredients for the drink in a cocktail shaker (apart from the chorizo!), add ice and shake well. Strain into the prepared glass and serve with chorizo on the side.

MELON & CUCUMBER WATER
Separately juice 75g (2¾oz) watermelon and 25g (scant 1oz) cucumber, then strain both. Blend together and use on the same day.

CHALLA-DAYS!

Andrew Gressman, Palenque Mezcaleria
Denver, USA

GLASS: COUPE

30ml (1fl oz) *raicilla* or mezcal
15ml (½fl oz) Hendrick's gin
30ml (1fl oz) apple juice
15ml (½fl oz) cranberry juice
15ml (½fl oz) pure agave nectar
15ml (½fl oz) lime juice
2 tsp cranberry shrub
orange zest strip studded with cloves, to garnish

Shake the first six ingredients together with ice,
then strain into a coupe glass and stir in the
cranberry shrub. Garnish with the clove-studded
orange zest. That's it! Easy as ABC.

TOMMY'S MARGARITA

Julio Bermejo, Tommy's
San Francisco, USA

GLASS: MARGARITA, OR ANY YOU LIKE

60ml (2fl oz) 100% agave tequila
30ml (1fl oz) lime juice
15ml (½fl oz) pure agave nectar

Shake the ingredients over ice. Strain into a
glass. Add ice and a lime wedge, if you like.

MEZCAL SOUR WITH ROSE PEPPER

Kristoffer Piilgaard Porner, Mesteren & Lærlingen
Copenhagen, Denmark

Any mezcal will do. Just be careful not to 'kill' the flavour notes in a small-batch blended mezcal with the lime and pepper. The mezcal should be the main focus… the sweet-and-sour part is to even it out and make it more easily approachable.

GLASS: COUPE

50ml (1¾fl oz) mezcal, preferably *espadin*
35ml (1¼fl oz) Rose Pepper Syrup (see below)
2 tbsp lime juice
2 tsp egg whites
1 big (or 2 small) dash(es) of Angostura bitters
freshly crushed pink peppercorns, to garnish

Shake all the ingredients together to get a foam. Add ice and shake again to cool and mix. Fine-strain into a coupe glass (or whatever you've got lying around) and sprinkle with crushed pink pepper.

ROSE PEPPER SYRUP

Dry-fry 2 tbsp pink peppercorns until they smell aromatic, but don't burn them. Take them off the heat, crush the peppercorns, then tip into a saucepan. Add 500ml (18fl oz/generous 2 cups) water, 250g (9oz/1¼ cups) granulated sugar and ½ tbsp distilled white vinegar. Bring it to the boil, stirring until the sugar has dissolved, then cool and strain. This makes more than you need, but will keep for up to one month in the fridge.

RAICILLA MARTINI

Chris Wingate, Palenque Mezcaleria
Denver, USA

GLASS: MARTINI
a little Dolin dry white vermouth
60ml (2fl oz) *raicilla* or mezcal
30ml (1fl oz) Hendrick's gin
2 tsp green olive brine
2 stuffed green olives, ideally stuffed with cheese, to garnish

Rinse a martini glass with the vermouth. Shake or stir all the other liquid ingredients together with ice, then strain into the glass.

Add the green olives last, then serve.

PEDAS MARGARITA

Dre Masso, Akademi
Bali, Indonesia

GLASS: MARTINI

a few dried hibiscus blossoms,
    crushed (optional)
sea salt
caster (superfine) sugar
40ml (1½fl oz) *reposado* mezcal
20ml (¾fl oz) coconut arak
50ml (1¾fl oz) pineapple purée
20ml (¾fl oz) lime juice
15ml (½fl oz) Chilli (Chile) Syrup (see below)
dried orange and lime slices, to garnish

Make a rim on a martini glass with the
hibiscus, if using, salt and sugar (see
page 190). Shake together all the liquid
ingredients over ice, then strain into the
prepared glass. Garnish with dried orange
and lime slices.

CHILLI (CHILE) SYRUP
To make chilli (chile) syrup, blend 1 small red
chilli (chile), including seeds, with 250ml
(9fl oz/generous 1 cup) Sugar Syrup (see
page 213). Strain into a bottle. This makes
more than you need, but will keep for up to
one month in the fridge.

EL OTRO VERDE

Nathan Schmit, Palenque Mezcaleria
Denver, USA

GLASS: ROCKS
40ml (1½fl oz) *raicilla* or mezcal
40ml (1½fl oz) grappa
orange slices, to serve
sal de gusano, to serve

Mix the *raicilla* and grappa and serve with ice cubes. Offer orange slices sprinkled with *sal de gusano,* or make a rim of *sal de gusano* (see page 190) and add an orange wedge.

MAGRONI

Phil Bayly, Agave Love
Sydney, Australia

GLASS: LARGE ROCKS
30ml (1fl oz) *espadin* mezcal
30ml (1fl oz) Antico Formula red vermouth
30ml (1fl oz) Campari
twist of orange zest

Add all the liquid ingredients to a mixing glass with ice and stir… not too much as you don't want to over-dilute the drink! Strain into a chilled large rocks glass over a large ice ball or cubes. Garnish with the orange zest.

TO PLUM A SMOKE

Johann Wader, The Chug Club
Hamburg, Germany

GLASS: LARGE TUMBLER
60ml (2fl oz) *espadin* mezcal
25ml (scant 1fl oz) Plum Cordial (see below)
20ml (¾fl oz) lime juice
1 tsp absinthe
freshly ground black pepper

Shake all the liquid ingredients together, then pour into a tumbler with ice cubes and top with the black pepper.

PLUM CORDIAL

To make plum cordial, put 1kg (2lb 4oz) plums in a saucepan with 1kg (2lb 4oz) granulated sugar and 250ml (9fl oz/generous 1 cup) water. Bring to the boil, stirring to help dissolve the sugar, then remove from the heat, cover and allow to infuse for 24 hours. Strain, add 50ml (1¾fl oz) *blanco* tequila, then bottle and chill. This will keep for up to two weeks, and can be used for other cocktail needs.

[see previous page for recipe images, from left to right: El Otro Verde; Magroni; To Plum a Smoke

BIENVENIDOS

Karl Wrangel, The Barking Dog
Copenhagen, Denmark

GLASS: MARTINI

40ml (1½fl oz) *espadin* mezcal, or to taste

20ml (¾fl oz) Kahlua

20ml (¾fl oz) lime juice, or to taste,
    plus a twist of lime zest, to garnish

Stir the ingredients over ice and serve straight up, with the twist of lime zest. Please feel free to tweak the recipe to suit the mezcal you're using.

DIXIBEE *LEMON-CHIPOTLE MARGARITA*

Nick Peters, Mamasita
Melbourne, Australia

GLASS: TALL GIBRALTAR
sea salt
60ml (2fl oz) mezcal (we are currently using Alipús)
45ml (1½fl oz) lemon juice
½ tsp chipotle paste
½ tsp tamarind purée
1 tsp pure agave nectar
nutmeg, to garnish
2 lemon wedges, to garnish

Wet the rim of a tall Gibraltar glass, then place into a saucer of sea salt, to create an evenly salted rim.

Shake all the remaining ingredients over ice and strain into the prepared glass. Grate over some nutmeg and serve with the lemon wedges.

THE SPICY RAICI

Chris Wingate, Palenque Mezcaleria
Denver, USA

GLASS: ROCKS
sea salt
30ml (1fl oz) *raicilla* or mezcal
30ml (1fl oz) pure agave nectar
chai beer

Use the salt to make a salt rim on a rocks glass (see left).

Add ice cubes to the glass and pour over the *raicilla* and agave nectar. Stir together, then top up with chai beer.

RAICILLA BATANGA

Nathan Schmidt, Palenque Mezcaleria
Denver, USA

This is the way it is done in many parts of Jalisco, and my absolute favourite.

Put ice cubes in a Collins glass and add a healthy pinch of salt. Pour in the *raicilla* and lime and top up with Coca-Cola to taste. Serve with a slice of lime.

GLASS: COLLINS
healthy pinch of sea salt
45ml (1½fl oz) *raicilla*, or pungent mezcal
juice of ½ lime, plus lime slice, to garnish
Coca-Cola, ideally Mexican Coca-Cola

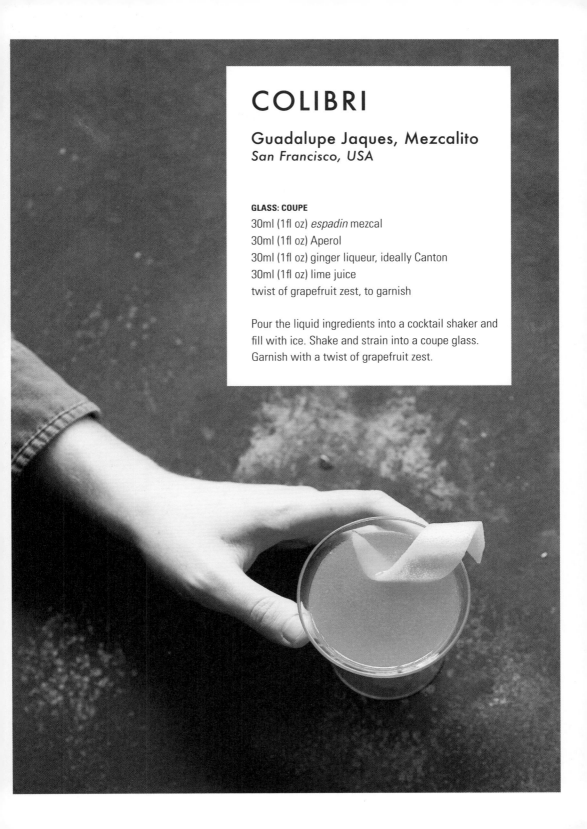

COLIBRI

Guadalupe Jaques, Mezcalito
San Francisco, USA

GLASS: COUPE

30ml (1fl oz) *espadin* mezcal
30ml (1fl oz) Aperol
30ml (1fl oz) ginger liqueur, ideally Canton
30ml (1fl oz) lime juice
twist of grapefruit zest, to garnish

Pour the liquid ingredients into a cocktail shaker and
fill with ice. Shake and strain into a coupe glass.
Garnish with a twist of grapefruit zest.

CAMINO

Jeremy Blackmore, Tio's Cerveceria
Surry Hills, Australia

GLASS: OLD-FASHIONED

40ml (1½fl oz) *blanco* tequila
20ml (¾fl oz) Tamarind Syrup (see below)
2 tsp lime juice
1 tbsp egg white
twist of lime zest, to garnish
freshly cracked black pepper, to garnish

Combine the tequila, syrup, lime juice and egg white in a
cocktail shaker. Shake and strain into an old-fashioned glass
over ice. Serve with a twist of lime zest and a sprinkling of
cracked black pepper.

TAMARIND SYRUP

To make tamarind syrup, blend 1 tbsp tamarind paste with
500ml (18fl oz/generous 2 cups) Sugar Syrup (see page 213).
Strain into a bottle. This makes more than you need, but will
keep for up to one month in the fridge.

CUCUMBER GINGER HIGHBALL

Espita bar team, Espita
Washington, DC, USA

GLASS: HIGHBALL
40ml (1½fl oz) *espadin* mezcal
20ml (¾fl oz) lime juice
20ml (¾fl oz) Cucumber-ginger Syrup (see below)
125ml (4fl oz/½ cup) soda water
long, thin cucumber slice, to garnish

Add ice cubes to a highball glass, then pour in each of the ingredients. Give the drink a light stir with a straw. Roll the cucumber slice, secure with a cocktail stick and use it as a garnish.

CUCUMBER-GINGER SYRUP

In a tightly sealed jar, shake together 100ml (3½fl oz/7 tbsp) cucumber juice, 20ml (¾fl oz) ginger juice, and 100g (3½oz/½ cup) caster (superfine) sugar until the sugar has dissolved. (To juice the ginger and cucumber, use a juicer or a blender. If using the latter, add a little water to the ginger before blending. Strain each juice through a fine-meshed sieve/strainer.) This makes more than you need, but will keep in the fridge for up to two weeks.

MACUSA

Fernando Suelo, Tentacion
Berlin, Germany

We named this cocktail after our dog, who we named after the Compay Segundo song of ultimate love.

GLASS: HIGHBALL
2 tsp aged mezcal
40ml (1½fl oz) young (*joven*) mezcal
80ml (3fl oz) cloudy apple juice
30ml (1fl oz) apple liqueur
2 tsp almond syrup
2 tsp lemon juice
dried lime slice, to garnish

Mix all the ingredients together with ice cubes, then strain into a glass. Garnish with the dried lime slice.

THE GOOD LIAR

Beckaly Franks (inspired by Miyako Kai), The Pontiac
Hong Kong

GLASS: OLD-FASHIONED

30ml (1fl oz) Cointreau
15ml (½fl oz) Alipús San Baltazar mezcal
15ml (½fl oz) lime juice
1 tsp Sugar Syrup (see right)
10 mint leaves
8–10 dashes of Peychaud's bitters
twist of orange zest, to garnish

Shake the first five ingredients together, then double-strain over ice cubes into the vessel of your choice, or an old-fashioned glass. Float the bitters on top and garnish with a twist of orange zest.

SUGAR SYRUP

To make this, just put two parts granulated sugar and one part water in a saucepan and gently heat, stirring until all the sugar has dissolved. Pour the syrup into a clean bottle and it's ready to use. This will keep for up to one month in the fridge.

JANE DOE

Mike Tomasic, Rhonda's
Terrigal, Australia

GLASS: OLD-FASHIONED

30ml (1fl oz) Del Maguey Minero mezcal,
   infused with ancho chilli/chile (see right)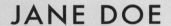
30ml (1fl oz) Amaro
30ml (1fl oz) oloroso sherry
1 tsp pure agave nectar
dashes of Bittermens Xocolatl Mole bitters
twist of orange zest, to garnish

Stir all the ingredients together and strain
into an old-fashioned glass filled with ice
cubes. Garnish with a twist of orange zest.

Serve with a wink and a smile.

ANCHO CHILLI (CHILE) MEZCAL

Pour mezcal into a jam jar and drop in one or
two dried ancho chillies (chiles). Seal the jar
and place in a cool, dark place for four days.
Taste. If you want more chilli (chile) flavour,
re-seal and leave for another day or so, until
it's right for you. Strain.

MEZCAL DIABLO

The staff, La Clandestina
Mexico City, Mexico

GLASS: NO GLASS!
1 large hot red chilli (chile)
175ml (6fl oz/¾ cup) Enmascarado 54 mezcal

Slice off the top of the chilli (chile), pour in some of the mezcal and sip. The longer one takes to finish this, the more the mezcal reacts with the flavours and spice of the chilli (chile), becoming increasingly more delicious, complex as well as hot.

MANZANA DEL MAR

Les Frye, Voodoo Café
Darlington, UK

GLASS: COUPE
30ml (1fl oz) Papadiablo Especial mezcal
25ml (scant 1fl oz) Calvados
20ml (¾fl oz) Licor 43
20ml (¾fl oz) lime juice
20ml (¾fl oz) caramel syrup
1 tsp Enmascarado 54 mezcal
slice(s) of apple, to garnish

Shake all the ingredients except the Enmascarado 54 together and pour into a coupe glass. Top with the Enmascarado 54. Serve with an apple slice, or a fan of apple slices, as you prefer.

EL PURO-PURO

The author, Mezcal Circle Club International
The Universe

GLASS: SMALL WIDE-MOUTHED CUP
60ml (2fl oz) Papadiablo Especial mezcal
15 minutes of free time

Take a quiet room, add some low lighting, switch off all electronic devices and, into a small, wide-mouthed *copita*, pour the Papadiablo Especial. Settle into your favourite chair, sip and consider the wonder of the material domain in which you momentarily exist.

LAST CALL

One batch to the next, a bottle over time, one cup — with the weather, the company, the location, even just with yourself — mezcal is always changing. And so it is with mezcal culture as a whole. Right now, faster than ever before.

Its new celebration worldwide has placed unprecedented pressure on the traditions and the communities that uphold them. There is a risk that, through our enthusiasm, we may alter the thing we fell in love with. One way to avoid this is to keep informed. Two great websites to help are mezcalistas.com and mezcalphd.com.

Another way is to go out and spread clear and accurate information about mezcal. Debunk the myths. After all, when mezcal does find us, it has the curious knack of creating in us all an agave ambassador.

~

I'd like to recount something my friend, movie-maker Matt Anderson, movingly blurted to me. 'To craft with your hands is meditation. To work in a group is community. Every part of making mezcal is a ceremony. Your day becomes, in its way, a prayer.' When we turn away from community and the relationship between people and land, plant and product, we create a relationship of ownership, which is unsustainable. The end of that road is every man for himself. The plants will no longer take care of us.

There can be no 'ownership' in mezcal. *Mezcaleros* talk of the plants and the land and the drink itself as something larger than the sum of the parts. It belongs to all of us, and we are equally responsible for its wellbeing, if not its survival. The least we can do is our part. If you're able, visit the regions where it is made and see how your choices make a difference. Or, at home, aim for mezcals that won't corrode the culture. If they are more pricey, we ought to adjust ourselves to that, rather than expect to bend the culture to our budget. Treat mezcal as it is, a treasure.

~

Last call. I met a chap just now, parked outside my apartment in Mexico City. He's driving a VW camper from Argentina to Alaska. He started his journey four years ago, just as mezcal was beginning to boom. He told me he's discovering the purpose of the journey as he goes. Maybe there's a higher purpose to mezcal's emergence right now. Something we can learn from the way it's made and the people that make it. Perhaps even from the spirit itself. *Aho.*

GLOSSARY

ABV Percentage of alcohol by volume. Traditionally, in mezcal, around 45% and up.

Agave The *materia prima* of mezcal. A succulent, not a cactus and – as a genus – in possession of perhaps more applicable uses for mankind than any other plant on earth.

Agua miel Sweet sap from specific agaves; a nutritious beverage which, left to ferment, becomes *pulque* (see right).

Alembic A type of still directly derived from an Arabic second-century design.

Añejo Mezcal or tequila that, to add flavour, is aged in barrels for at least twelve months.

Bacanora Regional name for Sonoran mezcal made using *Agave pacifica*, a variant of *espadin*.

Bagasso Fibrous pulp of the cooked agave, useful around the *palenque*.

Bulbos Bulbs of baby budding agave, dropped from the plant to root.

Campesino The 'little man', as opposed to big business.

Capon The practice of, for the benefit of maximum sugars, cutting the flower stem of the agave before it seeds and leaving it to stand in the earth for up to several years.

Conejo Literally 'rabbit', and used to describe dodgy distillates.

Copita Wide-mouthed gourd cup.

CRM or **COMERCAM** The agency in charge of overseeing the DO for mezcal.

Cuioté / quiote The central stem of the agave that, just once in an agave's life-cycle, rises as a trunk from its centre to release its seeds, flowers and *bulbos*.

Curado Mezcal infused with medicinal herbs, or any traditional medicine.

Curandera Mexican shaman.

Damajuana Clay pot or glass jug (pitcher) for holding mezcal. Typically a gallon or five litres, it was counted as a 'measure', a *medida*, and is the way mezcal was stored, sold and transported in the past.

Denominación de Origen Internationally recognized classification system meant to protect a culinary product – be it wine, cheese, honey, ham or spirits – that has unique cultural value.

Dexeebe Zapotecan toast, not uncommon in Oaxaca.

Espadin Predominant agave in Oaxaca, relatively quick and easy to grow and with ample sugars.

Garrafón Bottle – can be glass but usually plastic – to hold water or mezcal; these are everywhere at the *palenque*. The glass variety are buried underground in some regions to allow the spirit to 'rest'.

Hijuelos Clonal shoots shot from between the base and the root system of an agave equipped for this sort of procreation.

Jaice The Judge. The person designated to pour mezcal for a group for an evening.

Jimador Person who cuts or harvests the agave in Jalisco and other regions.

Karwinskii Name attributed to a venerated agave species by 19th-century German botanist, Wilhelm Friedrich Karwinskii.

Maguey Ancient Antillean word for agave, brought to Mexico by the Spanish and in common use today.

Mamposteria Steam oven introduced in the nineteenth century for cooking agave.

Mezcalero/a A person who makes mezcal,

or loves, lives for and understands mezcal.

Mezcaleria A place where we drink mezcal.

Molina Literally a 'mill'. In the world of mezcal, it's the part of the *palenque* where the cooked agave is ground.

Nahua Aztec language. The early form of Nuhuatl.

NOM Norma Oficial Mexicana (Official Mexican Standard), abbreviated to NOM, the name of each of a series of official, compulsory standards and regulations for diverse activities in Mexico.

Ordinario Meaning 'ordinary' as in not-jazzy-just-yet, it is the mezcal off the first distillation of a double distillation production and thus low in alcohol. Also called *shishe*.

Otomi People of contemporary Puebla, Guanajuato and Michoacán, with an ancient relationship to the agaves of those regions.

Palenque Colloquial name for a mezcal distillery in the South of Mexico.

Paz, Octavio Mexican poet and intellectual and writer of *The Labyrinth of Solitude*, seen by many as the most accomplished explanation of the Mexican psyche.

Pechuga Triple-distilled mezcal, with a flavouring – usually a local fruit or meat – added for the last round.

Penca The leaves of an agave.

Perlas Bubbles created in a spirit upon shaking, precisely indicating its ABV.

Piñas The heart of the agave and the part roasted to make mezcal. The word means 'pineapple', as they resemble one.

Pulque Fermented agave sap, a milky, viscous, alcoholic fluid.

Puntas The first part of a second distillation and thus high in ABV, between 60 and 80%.

Traditionally used to bring the mezcal to measure, it's also a 'delicacy' and its own kind of high.

Raicilla A Jaliscan mezcal made using plants endemic to the region.

Refrescadora A device that allows mezcal to be made from a single distillation.

Reposado Mezcal that is aged in barrels, to add colour and flavour to the spirit.

Sal de gusano The spicy salts of myriad recipes and indispensable to Southern Mexican cuisine. These days, sprinkled over orange slices to be served alongside mezcals as a nice freshener-upper.

Silvestre A wild variety of agave.

Sotol Spirits made using sotol plants in the states of Chihuahua, Durango and Coahuila.

Tahona A giant stone wheel, weighing several tons, used in mezcal production to crush cooked agave, dragged by a mule.

Tiña Fermentation vat, made from a variety of materials.

Yegolé Region in Oaxaca where prized mezcals are made.

Zapotec Enchanting language of the Zapotecan people that call parts of Oaxaca their home. Mezcal and the Zapotecan people are strongly connected.

INDEX

ACKNOWLEDGEMENTS

By small way of thank you, I'd like to acknowledge the generous efforts and sharing of time, information, resources and advice from the following people:

Alan Ibarra, Meredith Dreiss, Tom Estes, Dylan Sloan, Alejandro Gamez, Jonathan Barbieri, Héctor Vázquez, Silvia Philion, David Castillo, Ulises y Sandra, Karla Moles, Memo Hernández y su familia, Reina Sanchez, Humberto Dueñas, Hugo D'Acosta, Pedro Quintilla, Sanzekan, Nils Dallmann, Jason Cox, Karl Lenin, Dre Masso, Axel Huhn, my editors Lucy Bannell, Fritha Saunders, Rachel Cross and the helpful assistants at Quarto. Anna Bruce, Eddie Ruscha, Alberto Cruz, Cody Copeland, Anders Selmer, Iñes y Carlos, Brilliant Corners and everyone at the brands and bars who contributed as well as the many *mezcaleros y mezcaleras* who welcomed me into their homes.

I'd also like to thank the family and friends who directly made this possible, particularly my brother Lofty, my Dad, Jake Singer, Kyle and Kellen, Tim 'Luz' Lee and The Hunts.

And now, in true B-Boy style, I'd like to give a shout out to all the people that helped make this recording happen along the way...

Cousin Josh, Bee, Sista Dwoo and my champion nephew George, Big Brother Jay, Caro and the kids, Matt Kenney, JB, Brother Bix and Claire aussi, Fergs and Rebs, Eugene and Max, Heidi and Andrew, Lady Cundra, Brother Harvwah, Guido B, DJ 2 Grand, Eric 'LP' D, Lani and Brett, Flabby Abbs and Gordon and The Girls, my wicked uncles and 'The Greater Herd', Gary and Neive, Moseph, Adia and Baby Bayou, Garth, Markie and Jeno, Lisa and Loz, Zoe B, Shan and Moon, Paul Simonon, A Rose, Paul T, Stevie G, Chris Novi, Mr Dan Mitchell, my Uncle Bill, Thomas Sandbichler and family, Daryl and Cheri, Kevie Kev, The Ruschas, Jill Kennedy and Noble Fine, The QuiQuiRiQui Girls, Nathan C, The Georgia Massive, As Four, Commend in the place, Sister Lils, Gavin Brown, my Druids, Big Game James, 2 Many DJs, The '2 Much Pressure' Patels, Dave I.D., The Magnificent Henry B, Bobbie Marie, Chebon, The Mighty P.A.M. Crew, Dope Jams Posse, Rob Brezny, Jerry 'The Godfather' Heller, Pistol Pete, Gigi La Peu, Alexis Gordon – we miss you, Andee, Naut Humon, CB, Phil Bayly, House de Frost, Nomads Phil, Darking, Luke Stidworthy, The Straight As, S.S., Giles Folden, Patrick @ Duke's, Charlie Uzzel, Sister Ev, Papa D Crew, Jaime and Gustavo, Alvin Starks, Jair Tellez, Jesse Estes, Jason and Carlos at El Destilado, Thea 'Moon Unit' Cumming, Thomasina Miers, A Ron, Shoppie and Michal, Tom Bartram, Jon Anders, everyone at Coe Vintners, Reed, Osamu-Raj, Whatty and the JP Crew, Limited Edition, Alex Olson, Kirsten Baughy, M de B, Quinny and fam, Lee from The Top, and the staff at Alvaros Tacos, Oaxaca.

This book is dedicated to Owl and Nibs, Dad and Uma and all the lot from down The Green.

Good session, good session.

MEZCALERIA PHOTOGRAPHY pp106–7, pp120–1, p123 and p126 courtesy of Mezcaloteca; p109 courtesy of Archivo Maguey; p111 Silvia Gin; p112 courtesy of Espita; p113 and p133 courtesy of Bar Clandestino; p113 courtesy of Del 24 Taqueria, Tentacion; p117 courtesy of Gallo Pélon; p118 © tRm/Flickr; p125 courtesy of Oppa-La; p126 courtesy of Brahms & Liszt, Bad Sports; p127 courtesy of La Mezcaleria; p128 courtesy of Pare de Sufrir; p130 courtesy of Super Loco; p132 courtesy of The Barking Dog, Sacapalabras, Tio's Cerveceria.

ILLUSTRATIONS Alberto Cruz Perez pages 1, 6, 11, 16–7, 36–7, 58–61, 64–5, 66–7, 70, 90, 96–7, 134–5, 184–5, 219, 220–1, 222–3, 224; **Eddie Ruscha Jr** pages 46–53, 56–7.

ALL OTHER PHOTOGRAPHY
Annika Boerm: page 85 (top). **Bridgeman Images**: p28.

Anna Bruce: pages 12 top left and right, middle left and centre, bottom centre; 13 top left, middle left, bottom centre; 21; 43 top left; middle centre, bottom left; 63 top centre and right, middle left and centre; 68 top right and centre, middle left, bottom left; 69 bottom left; 71; 72–3; 74; 75; 76; 83; 87; 99; 105; 183. **Tom Bullock**: pages 7; 8; 12 top centre, middle right, bottom left and right; 13 top right, middle centre and right, bottom left; 14; 15; 19; 23; 25; 29; 35; 39; 40; 41; 43 top right; 62 top left, middle left and right, bottom right; 63 top left, and all bottom of page; 68 top right, middle right, bottom centre and right; 69; 78; 81; 85 (bottom); 89; 91; 109; 128; 181. **Uma Bullock**: page 13 bottom right. **Kyle Garner**: page 63, middle right. **Alan Ibarra**: pages 2; 3; 4; 5; 13 top centre; 27; 31; 43 bottom; 54–5; 62 top centre, bottom centre; 86; 93; 95. **Zorana Musikic**: page 68 middle centre.